HOLDING MY FATHER'S HAND: FAITH-BASED PARENTING

By

Pamela J. Bradley, EdD

All Scripture quotations marked NKJV are taken from the *New King James Version* of the Bible. Copyright © 1979, 1980, 1982, Thomas Nelson, Inc., Publishers.

All Scripture quotations marked ESV are taken from *The Holy Bible, English Standard Version*. Copyright © 2001 by Crossway Bibles, a division of Good News Publishers.

All Scripture quotations marked NLT are taken from the *Holy Bible, New Living Translation*, copyright © 1996. Used by permission of Tyndale House Publishers, Inc., Wheaton, Illinois 60189. All rights reserved.

Holding My Father's Hand: Faith-based Parenting
Copyright © 2015 by Pam Bradley
ISBN: 978-1-942451-07-5
Email: pambradley7@gmail.com
or bradley.pamela7@yahoo.com
Website: pambradley.net

Published by Yorkshire Publishing, LLC
9731 East 54th Street
Tulsa, OK 74146

Cover Photo: Mayra Ruiz-Valtierra
Text Design: Lisa Simpson

Printed in the United States. All rights are reserved under International Copyright Law. Contents and/or cover may not be reproduced in whole or in part in any form without the express prior written consent of Pamela J. Bradley.

Dedication

This book is dedicated to my sweet hubby, Charles, who has served as my parenting partner for the past twenty-three years, *and* to my five children: Jeremy, Bekie, Cali, Archie, and Alex. What a blessing you are!

Thank-Yous to:

Our Lord and Father, who made all things possible and inspired me to write this book! Maudye Winget, my friend who added creative eloquence to my words; Dianne Haralson, who served as an expert editor; My husband, Charles and my five children, Jeremy, Rebecca (Bekie), Cali, Archie and Alex for their unconditional love; My sisters, Hope, Phyllis, Paula, Karen and Sharon, who encouraged me; Numerous friends and extended family who serve as my village, and all who provided suggestions and participated in the parenting survey.

Background

Throughout this book, I make several references to the various phases of my life. The information here provides a chronological order for the reader.

After graduating high school and attending a semester of college, I married my high school sweetheart. During this marriage, I finished college, obtained employment as a teacher and gave birth to three beautiful children, Jeremy, Bekie and Cali. Nine years later, in an attempt to salvage my marriage, I quit my job. That effort failed, and I soon found myself a single, unemployed mother of three.

Back in the teaching force, I secured a master's degree in school administration to better support my family. After almost five years as a single parent, I remarried. Charles, the once-confirmed bachelor, stepped bravely into his new role as a step-dad, blending our family. Eighteen months into our marriage, I gave birth to Archie, and just two years later, Alex followed. Our hearts and home continue to be full of love as our children teach us much and God guides us on this amazing, difficult, but rewarding journey.

Table of Contents

Foreword 9

Preface 11

Introduction 17

Chapters

1 The Nonnegotiables 19
     God First 20
     Unconditional Love 26

2 Village People 33

3 Master Your Monsters (and I Don't Mean the Kids!) 45

4 Let There BE (Boundaries and Expectations) 55

5 Make Moments to Remember 71

6 Shining Beyond the Diamond 81

7 Blended Blessings 97

8 The Ongrowing Journey 113

Appendix 123

Resources/References 131

Foreword
by Maudye Winget

Pam Bradley's story is the journey of a great American family! She writes about her highest parenting highs and her lowest lows with great conviction. One thing the reader will come to understand is that a parent (whether single or with a partner) can help shape the course of her children's lives through prayer and listening. Pam Bradley is a high energy, proactive person who took the time to listen to her children, all five of whom are successful in their own right. Pam uses scripture as the basis for her decision making not only in life in general, but in particular as she parented her children as a married parent, as a single parent and during the last 24 years in partnership with her husband, Charles. Pam's story is fascinating and offers hope for those who feel stuck in the throes of being a parent. Believe me, you will enjoy getting to know Pam, her husband, and their five children: Jeremy, Beki, Cali, Archie and Alex.

Maudye Winget
Recipient of the Oklahoma Foundation
for Excellence Medal of Excellence in
School Administration Award 1998;
Oklahoma Arts Alliance Administrator of the Year Award 1998;
Readers Digest Hero in American Education Award 1999,
and the Governor's Arts Award 1999

Preface

"Train up a child in the way he should go; even when he is old he will not depart from it."

Proverbs 22:6 ESV

As parents, we do what we know. If we don't know better, that's all we can do. At the tender age of 19, when I became a parent, that's what I did. Using my parents as a model—the good, the bad, and the ugly—I did only what I knew.

It wasn't long before I recognized that much of what I was doing wasn't right … it wasn't working. I began to search for an instructional manual on parenting—and found it in God's word. Still, it was my task to study it, pray about it, and apply it. Not just for parenting … but for life. This required a concerted effort on my part to create different habits.

Throughout my thirty-seven years as a parent, I've grown and changed. Surviving a divorce, five years of parenting alone, a second marriage plus the birth of two more children, and breast cancer, my thoughts about parenting have undergone a major shift. I've always said, "It's okay not to know, but it's not okay not to grow." I'm still growing.

This is my story, which includes faith-based practices developed along the way. I've made many mistakes, but through them, I've evolved into a different person … a healthier parent. What I've learned thus far is though I may have influenced my children, it was I who ultimately was changed for the better.

LISTENING TO GOD

After choosing to retire as a public school principal, I was called to a new journey. Not that what I did wasn't important anymore; it is just that God tugged me in another direction.

I wasn't quite sure what that would be at the time, but I prayed and felt the first tug as God began to answer, guiding me on an indirect two-year path to get here. *Write. Write a book*, He seemed to be saying. After all, I had been talking about writing a book for years. It was a dream of mine—and now it seemed a directive from God.

"About what?" I asked. I had three ideas in my head, three stories to write—but which first? I polled my sisters, children, hubby, and a few friends. I prayed hard. God's answer began to unfold: *Parenting*. But that's not what my sisters said. *Parenting*, I heard again. But that's not what my friends said. *Parenting*, I heard a third time in my heart. But that's not what my hubby said. When I heard it a fourth time, there was no doubt where God was leading me.

Parenting? Yeah—I know quite a bit about that. As a mother of five very distinctly different individuals, one of eight siblings, aunt to twenty-three, and teacher and principal to thousands of children, I have a pretty good understanding of, as well as valuable experience in, the realm of parenting.

After all, becoming a parent can be easy. You either give birth, adopt, or inherit another human being. Yet, being a parent is much harder—children don't come with instructions.

Preface

I had my reservations and I shared them with God. These reservations actually became full-blown excuses. "I have made a lot of mistakes as a parent, Lord. I mean A LOT of mistakes. I'm not sure where to start or what to include in this book."

"Yes, you did make a lot of mistakes—but you learned from those mistakes. It's true that you don't have all the answers. No one does, but I will guide you in this process. No, you don't know where to start, but step out in faith and begin. Just do it."

It seemed that God was spurring me on. Still, I hesitated, realizing perhaps that I shouldn't write about a subject I myself had not mastered.

Despite many years of service in several arenas—teacher, principal, wife, sister, friend, mother—my experiences left me lacking. As I gave consideration to the subject of parenting, it dawned on me that no matter how you looked at it, I had a long way to grow in all capacities. But I also grasped that my thirty-seven years of experience might help someone avoid some of the pitfalls I had already worked through.

As I attempted to wrap my head (and heart) around the incredible responsibility of parenting, I realized parenting is the most significant role in all of life—despite the fact that it is also possibly the most unappreciated, undercompensated (unless you count sloppy kisses and bear hugs), undertrained, and unmonitored job in the world. Regarding the wide influence of parents, Haim G. Ginott (1993) wrote:

I have come to the frightening conclusion that I am the decisive element. It is my personal approach that creates the climate. It is my daily mood that makes the weather. I possess tremendous power to make life miserable or joyous. I can be a tool of torture or an instrument of inspiration. I can humiliate or humor. In all situations, it is my response that decides whether a crisis is escalated or de-escalated, and a person is humanized or de-humanized. If we treat people as they are, we make them worse. If we treat people as they ought to be, we help them become what they are capable of becoming.

Parents have the potential to do real damage. Allow the reality and enormity of that to sink in. There is no greater assignment in all the world. Seriously.

It's odd then that we might approach parenting using a fly-by-the-seat-of-our-pants method, with little thought and unintended carelessness. Perhaps because humans have been parenting for thousands of years, we fail to home in on the magnitude of this role. We become oblivious to what's working and what's not ... or of what *really* matters as we parent!

With that in mind, I realized my purpose for this book is twofold. First, to convey the significance of this role so that other parents and caregivers may choose to join me in working to get it right. Secondly, to provide a process for effective parenting using:

- Biblical principles and prayers
- Life-coaching strategies
- Research, as it relates to parenting

Preface

Directed in this mission, I realize there are no more excuses. It is time to write. Thus, I drive to my cabin on a rainy June morning, open my laptop, and after a long, hopeful prayer, I begin to type.

Introduction

Faith-based parenting: The process of promoting and supporting the physical, emotional, social, intellectual, and spiritual development of a child in partnership with God, using His Word as a foundation.

If you haven't yet noticed, parenting is the most rewarding, frustrating, challenging, fascinating, exhilarating, tearful, funny, exhausting, joyful, fulfilling, hair-pulling, and head-scratching role you will ever have. Many of us with strong-willed children have come to know this.

Since parents are often the most influential people in a child's life, this position can be quite scary. After all, parenting requires us to be *so* responsible. It causes us to feel *so* judged. It makes our actions *so* scrutinized. And, as a result, we often endure humiliation when our children's choices are seen as a reflection of us.

This blows my mind. It causes my heart to leap out of my chest. It twists my gut and sucks the wind out of my very essence as I consider the importance of parenting and how inept I may be at this job. After all, it is one thing to be responsible for my choices, which I can control. It's another thing to be responsible for other human beings who have minds, hearts, and spirits of their own, which I might influence, but I cannot necessarily control—despite my best efforts.

Gratefully, I have learned to depend on the only perfect parent, God. God knows best. Because He endowed us with an opportunity to shepherd these precious human beings into whom He meant them to be, He will provide us with resources: His word, His love, His guidance. As Psalms 27:3 says, *"Children are a gift from the Lord; they are a reward from him"* (NLT).

Though I wish I could offer a magic formula, I can't. There is no "one-size-fits-all" when it comes to working with children. It just doesn't exist. However, what I can share is a process that has worked for me. Through scriptures, coaching, research, and my own real experiences, I offer Biblical strategies to help you experience joy, growth, and reward as you navigate that bumpy road called parenting.

Chapter 1

THE NONNEGOTIABLES

"Do not be conformed to this world, but be transformed by the renewal of your mind, that by testing you may discern what is the will of God, what is good and acceptable and perfect."

Romans 12: 2 ESV

There are certain things in this life that are nonnegotiable. The most important being God's will. As I set out to establish my nonnegotiables for raising my children, I have come up with a short list through scriptures and prayer. These nonnegotiables are defined as "a way of being that is my bottom line—embedded in the very core of who I am." My "nonnegotiables" come from a philosophy which is firmly established and rooted in God's Word.

This framework provides parameters that guide my actions and decisions. They are the things that guide my way of *being* and *doing* as a parent. These are things that I cannot, will not budge on—because they are *that* essential … *that* necessary … *that* important.

My two nonnegotiables are:

- God first in my household; and
- unconditional love for my children

God First

"... choose this day whom you will serve ... But as for me and my house, we will serve the Lord."

Joshua 24:15 ESV

Let's begin with the first nonnegotiable. Why should we put God *first* in our lives? 2 Samuel 22:31 explains: *"This God—His way is perfect; the word of the Lord proves true; He is a shield for all those who take refuge in Him"* (ESV). The Bible says God's way is perfect, and that's enough for me.

Secondly, Matthew 22:37 says, *"You shall love the Lord with all your heart, and with all your soul and with all your mind"* (ESV). How do we, as parents, place God first in our lives? God first is a nice goal. It sounds good. It's easy to talk about, but what does it really mean? What does it look like in our households—in our lives?

Kurt Bruner (*Putting God First*) provides clarity, making faith-based parenting more visible and doable:

> Helping our children grow in their faith includes instilling habits of obedience. Our natural tendency is to neglect those practices that keep our relationship with God at the forefront of our hearts and minds. That's why it is important to

implement faith routines at home. Take children to worship services regularly. Pray with them before bed. Give each child an age-appropriate Bible to start him reading God's Word. At dinner, let each child describe the "high" and "low" moment of the day, then help her give thanks or seek guidance for those things. In short, make the idea of putting God first highly practical.

Bruner went on to say, "He [God] connected the dots between loving and doing when He said, 'If you love me, obey what I command'" (John 14:15 New International Version).

How do we love the Lord with all our heart, power, and might, while guiding our children to obey God's commandments so they may grow in the way that they should go?

My understanding is that in all things, including being a parent, we put God first. By putting God first, we infuse His words and His guidance in all areas of our lives, including—and most importantly—the area of parenting. And how does this impact our children? In all things, in all ways, at all times.

We use God's word and guidance to establish boundaries, expectations, discipline, and consequences for our children. We balance that by providing them with freedoms, responsibilities, and exposures to life. The scriptures help us to understand our role as parents, knowing we were meant to be our children's parents first, and our children's friends later.

Faith-based parenting is modeling, acting, and living in a way that is best for our children, even when it's not easiest for us. It means providing responsibilities for children and allowing them to learn what they need to know. It means taking time to actually explain and demonstrate how and why things should be done—from discipline to chores, play, respect, relationships, and more. If it relates to God, people, or good character, it should be taught and modeled.

As the Chinese proverb goes, "Give a man a fish and you feed him for a day. Teach a man to fish and you feed him for a lifetime." We must teach our children to fish, rather than just providing them with fish.

Teaching takes more time, and teaching is harder. It takes thought, planning, and direction. It takes paying attention and adjustments along the way. I liken it to being in a constant state of adjusting the sails on a stormy sea.

At times, we may find ourselves saying, "It's easier to just do it for them!" Be wary. This can send a message to our children that we don't trust or believe they are capable of doing something for themselves. According to Ann Dunnewold, PhD, a licensed psychologist and author of *Even June Cleaver Would Forget the Juice Box*, there are several unhealthy consequences that can come from such parenting:

- undeveloped coping skills
- increased anxiety
- sense of entitlement
- undeveloped life skills

The absence of life skills can lead to an unfulfilled life, a life that never reaches fruition, a life of self-absorption. We must show our children how the importance of sweat equity in a world of instant gratification contributes to the greater good, learning to appreciate people and feeling purposeful in life. As the scripture says, we must train them up in the way that they should go and trust that they will not depart from it.

In fact, it's important for us as parents to not only allow our children to learn, but, perhaps even more importantly, to allow them to fail in the process—and then require them to try again and again. This builds character traits such as persistence and tenacity. Challenges and difficulties can actually be good for our children, allowing them to not only build an arsenal of new skills, but to learn to deal effectively with future challenges.

As parents we must keep in mind that our children are capable, resilient beings, but we must help them further develop such traits. When we lower our expectations, we limit their self-efficacy and their future. We limit God.

Deuteronomy 6:9 says, "*6 And these words that I command you today shall be on your heart. 7 You shall teach them diligently to your children, and shall talk of them when you sit in your house, and when you walk by the way, and when you lie down, and when you rise. 8 You shall bind them as a sign on your hand, and they shall be as frontlets between your eyes. 9 You shall write them on the doorposts of your house and on your gates*" (ESV).

We must live our lives in a way that makes our children proud of us … in a way that makes them want to point us out as an example (excluding those middle school years when we suddenly become "uncool"). It means considering how our actions will affect our children, not just now but later down the road,

As parents, we live, share, and show our faith in a way that's tangible to our children. Though faith may be easy to talk about, the more complex part is the actual living in the faith—consistently. Our thoughts translate into words, our words into actions, our actions into habits, and our habits into our culture. Our culture becomes not only our way of being as a person, but, more often than not, our children's way of being as well.

Real Life Nonnegotiables: Alex

"... and a little child shall lead them."
Isaiah 11:6 ESV

I remember when my youngest son, Alex, was only three years old and I was holding his hand as I walked through the grocery store parking lot. His other chubby hand was raised up to the sky and his big brown eyes gazed upward to the clouds. Puzzled by his actions, I asked, "Alex, what in the world are you doing? Why are you holding out your hand?"

Alex stopped walking and looked from the clouds into my face, with a shake of his head, indignant at my ignorance. "Mom," he said. "I'm holding God's hand!"

The hairs on my arm stood on end, and chills ran up my spine. I saw in the angelic face of my young son a truth and faith like I had never witnessed before. This was a way of being for my son, and at this moment, he was teaching me.

The Nonnegotiables

Fast-forward twelve years to a high school locker room. Alex's football coach shared the following story ... Alex and his freshmen teammates were witness to a heated argument between a talented senior and a somewhat cocky sophomore. Egos were at stake, and the two young men were about to come to blows.

Sensing the tension, Alex stepped between them, his physical and emotional maturity obvious, even at the tender age of fifteen. "I know what you need," Alex said, breaking into a smile as his burly, bearded face squared with the younger man. "You need a hug!" Alex's muscular, hairy arms wrapped around his teammate, lifting him gently away from his opponent.

The whole team, including the sophomore and senior at odds, erupted into laughter, relieving the pressure building in the locker room. The boys shook hands and slapped backs. Alex's *being* had made the difference.

What is your way of being? How are you developing your child's way of being? How are you modeling righteousness, love, forgiveness, a good work ethic, responsibilities, resiliency, and a sense of fun and humor? Are your expectations appropriate and positive? Is your belief in your child evident? I'm not just talking Sunday School, Bible reading, scripture memorization, and conversations about God. I'm talking about a way of being, a way of talking and a way of treating others every single day. I'm talking about the culture of your family.

Parenting is a tall order, my friend, and I would love to tell you I get it right all the time. As a mother, I am a work in progress. Though I'm continually growing, there are still many speed bumps along the way. I often fail, and you will, too. After all, there is no perfect parent.

The key is to keep on keeping on. As Winston Churchill said in his famous speech in 1941, "Never give in. Never give in. Never, never, never, never—in nothing, great or small, large or petty—never give in, except to convictions of honour and good sense." With God's guidance, we will begin to get it right more often than not. And that is all the good Lord requires.

Unconditional Love

1 If I could speak in any language in heaven or on earth but didn't love others, I would only be making meaningless noise like a loud gong or a clanging cymbal. 2 If I had the gift of prophecy, and if I knew all the mysteries of the future and knew everything about everything, but didn't love others, what good would I be? And if I had the gift of faith so that I could speak to a mountain and make it move, without love I would be no good to anybody. 3 If I gave everything I have to the poor and even sacrificed my body, I could boast about it; but if I didn't love others, I would be of no value whatsoever. 4 Love is patient and kind. Love is not jealous or boastful or proud 5 or rude. Love does not demand its own way. Love is not irritable, and it keeps no record of when it has been wronged. 6 It is never glad about injustice but rejoices whenever the truth wins out. 7 Love never gives up, never loses faith, is always hopeful, and endures through every circumstance. 8 Love will last forever, but prophecy and speaking in unknown languages and special knowledge will all disappear."

1 Corinthians 13:1-8 NLT

The Nonnegotiables

These scriptures speak to the power and importance of love. As parents, there is no doubt that most of us have unconditional love for our children. And while we may love them forever and ever, it doesn't mean we approve of their actions. In fact, if we are really honest, there are times when we don't even like them.

This unconditional love means that no matter what our children do, they know that we will be there for them and beside them. It doesn't mean we condone or support all of their choices. It doesn't mean we get them "off the hook" or forgo consequences. It doesn't mean we accept inappropriate behaviors. As Proverbs19:22 tells us, "What a person desires is unfailing love …" (NIV).

On the other hand, loving our children unconditionally means that love isn't something our children have to earn. Rather, our love for them should be free and constant. Our children should feel loved for who they are, as we are willing to help them become who they were meant to be. It's not just about loving them when they're good, but also loving them when they aren't, when we are literally ready to give them away!

I've often heard divorced parents say, "I'm sending you back to live with your dad/mom. I can't deal with this!" In essence, what the child hears is, "I don't know if I can love you through this." I'm here to tell you that you can. It's a choice—albeit a tough one—that you must make for your child's sake.

It's much easier to "give our children away" or abandon them at the first sign, or any sign, of trouble. We should not demean them, we should not compare them to others, nor should we cut them off from all contact with us. In Luke 15:11-32, the Bible explains unconditional love through the Parable of the Prodigal Son. Below is a summary:

Jesus tells the story of a younger son requesting his inheritance early from his father, only to squander it all on a good time with his friends. Reduced to working with swine, the young man soon realizes how good his life had once been—how even the pigs eat better than he does, how even his father's servants have food and shelter. Despondent, destitute, humiliated, and remorseful, the prodigal chooses to return home, prepared to work as a servant for his father due to his poor choices. Instead, his father, who had been hoping and praying for the return of his son, forgives him and rejoices in his homecoming. Welcoming the prodigal with open arms, new sandals, a robe, and a ring, the father celebrates with a feast in his son's honor, demonstrating his unconditional love.

Just as the father in the prodigal son, we, too, should always offer our children unconditional love. This means that we believe in them (regardless of previous track records), foster the good in them, and always be present for them.

Offering unconditional love to my children means I must always pray for them and offer guidance as needed. I work to be the best example, modeling those things I am teaching, and living in a way that makes them proud to call me Mom. I provide consequences that I believe are best, even if this means my children may dislike, or even hate me for a while, recalling Psalm 30:5: *"For his anger lasts only a moment, but his favor lasts a lifetime! Weeping may last through the night, but joy comes with the morning"* (NLT).

The Nonnegotiables

In loving my children, I strive for balance both in my life and theirs. Though I take care of *their* needs, I must also take care of *my* needs; this is key to being a good parent. I am present for them—behind, beside, and before them—encouraging, nudging gently, and making sure they know they are loved and that I believe in them and see their best, no matter where they are in life.

On the other hand, I am not a doormat. I expect them to demonstrate love for me as their mother, show respect for my authority as a parent, and appreciate the wisdom that comes with my experience, age, and successes.

Just as Ephesians 6:1-3 says, *"Children, obey your parents in the Lord, for this is right. Honor your father and mother that it may go well with you and that you may live long ... "* (ESV).

Respect is a must! Yet, sometimes, even our nonnegotiables may conflict when we are called upon to make tough decisions. So, we must look to God for guidance and balance in this process.

For Christmas break his sophomore year of high school, Alex wanted to go with a church group to Mexico to work in an orphanage. Though burly, bearded, and much larger than me, Alex was still my baby. I'd heard horror stories on the news about Mexico being a dangerous place for Americans—drug cartels, homicides, tourist kidnappings, and more! Please understand that I love Alex more than my own life. I felt that if I said yes to the Mexico trip, his well-being could be jeopardized. I vehemently voiced my concerns and told him no.

Standing over me, Alex shook his head as I sat at the kitchen table drinking coffee and reading my morning devotional. "Mom, I've prayed about this, and I feel God is calling me to do this. I'll be in God's hands. I am being called to go to Mexico."

In essence, his message was, "God first, Mom. You taught us to listen to God's voice when He calls us to do something. Where's your faith?"

My heart jumped, and my pride blinded me for a moment. How dare he challenge me! I'm his mom. I'm the one who raised him to know God and have faith. Who was he to throw that back in my face?

An inner voice whispered in my head, *"You're not arguing with your son. You are arguing with God. Who are you to challenge me?"*

It blew my mind, but I knew this voice was from God, speaking to my ego and my heart. Alex was right. How could I argue with God? Where was my faith? God loved me enough to give me Alex. I trusted God enough to let go. Reluctantly, begrudgingly, and with misgivings and hopeful faith (an oxymoron, right?), I gave in and said "Yes. You're right. You can go." As Alex packed his bags, I packed my misgivings and moved out of his way.

As a parent, you, too, should determine your nonnegotiables. Realize that God put you in charge. Through Him, you have the skills and love to help shape your children into the people they were meant to be. That, my friend, is the most humbling assignment any person can be given.

The Nonnegotiables

Coaching Time

It's coaching time! Take out a pencil and paper, and find a quiet spot where you can seriously pray, reflect and respond to the following questions. My suggestion is to post your responses in a visible place so that you will be reminded of your parenting goals—your nonnegotiables, and celebrate your progress regularly. Remember, we measure and monitor what matters!

1. What are your nonnegotiables?

2. How would you define them?

3. How will you demonstrate and communicate your nonnegotiables as a parent to your children?

Because prayer is so vital to our lives, I want to include a brief description of this powerful connection we have with our Father. Prayer is simply a conversation with God. It is a way to glorify Him. It provides us an occasion to thank Him for our many blessings and to ask for help and guidance. This conversation allows us to cry out for comfort, peace, or joy whenever our hearts are thankful, weary, burdened, or hurting. God will hear. God will respond. God will direct.

All chapters end with this opportunity. Each prayer offered is my dialogue with God. Feel free to use my words or to call upon the Lord in your own way. No fancy speech required—just an honest, sincere, respectful exchange with the Lord. Prepare to receive as He responds in His time, in His way.

Prayer: *Lord, what are your nonnegotiables for me as a parent? In what ways can I serve you best in this privileged role as parent? Grant me the wisdom to discern your ways from the world as I wait for your response with an open mind and an open heart. Help my eyes to see and my ears to hear your direction for me. In your name, I pray. Amen.*

Poem: I wrote this after giving birth to my firstborn, Jeremy.

The Soul of a Child

God gave me a seed, the soul of a child,
And said, "This gift is yours for awhile.
Take him and love him and raise him for me.
Provide a foundation of security.
Make sure he has Sonshine, guidance and care,
Discipline lovingly; always be there.
It'll take sacrifices, patience and time,
But he's very precious … remember, he's mine.
He'll follow your footsteps. He'll do as you do.
And when he grows up, he'll be quite like you.
So to nurture and guide this child so sweet,
I'll provide you a book with requirements to meet.
I promise my counsel, and strength I will share.
So, call on me often; I'll answer each prayer.
And then as God turned and started to go,
He reminded me firmly, "I'll come back, you know."
And when I return to reclaim my child,
I'll only take flowers, not weeds growing wild."

Chapter 2

Village People

> *"Two are better than one, because they have a good reward for their toil. For if they fall, one will lift up his fellow. But woe to him who is alone when he falls and has not another to lift him up! Again, if two lie together, they keep warm, but how can one keep warm alone? And though a man might prevail against one who is alone, two will withstand him—a threefold cord is not quickly broken."*
>
> Ecclesiastes 4:9-12 ESV

I read recently that raising children is entirely a parent's responsibility. I disagree. While the ultimate decisions and responsibilities rest with us, God has placed other people on this earth to help our children—and to help us in the process. That's something we must be mindful of. God doesn't expect us to do it alone.

> *"And let us consider how to stir up one another to love and good works, not neglecting to meet together, as is the habit of some, but encouraging one another, and all the more as you see the Day drawing near."*
>
> Hebrews 10:24-25 ESV

1 Peter 4:8-10 says, "*8 Above all, keep loving one another earnestly, since love covers a multitude of sins. 9 Show hospitality to one another without grumbling. 10 As each has received a gift, use it to serve one another, as good stewards of God's varied grace*" (ESV).

CHOOSING YOUR VILLAGE

Our village won't just happen. We must create it. We need to pray and ask God to help us *choose* our village—the right people who will love and support us. In return, we are also to *build* our village, meaning that we are to invest in these people as much as they invest in us (and our children). There are plenty of scriptures to support this notion. Philippians 2:4 tells us, *"Let each of you look not only to his own interests, but also to the interests of others"* (ESV).

1 Thessalonians 5:11 says, *"Therefore encourage one another and build one another up, just as you are doing"* (ESV).

Consider the people who should be in your village. Now consider the people who should be in your children's village. It may be that you choose different people for different purposes. Which people should you choose to encourage you as a person and parent? Which people should you choose to encourage your children? Some of these "village people" may overlap—falling into both categories. Others may only fall into one of those categories, and that's okay.

In the coaching section, we'll talk more about things to consider when choosing your village. Meanwhile, as you select and develop your village, as well as your children's, it's important to put any selfish, prideful, or unfair desires and emotions you may have aside. For example, if you are a single parent, and you know deep down that your ex-spouse has a positive influence on your children, you must allow and support that person as a part of your children's village, despite your feelings toward him or her. This is hard, but it must be done for the sake of your children.

On the other hand, you must do all you can to equip your children with the skills (physical, emotional, mental, and spiritual) to handle and overcome negative influences and/or people. As a parent, you must work harder than ever to surround your child with positive, Christian influences.

Another thing to consider in choosing and building your village is that sometimes, God puts people in our path to help us grow. Sometimes, God chooses people to be a part of our village that we might not have considered, and we must recognize and be discerning in this. Your village people can be school teachers, community leaders, grandparents, friends, or neighbors who offer sage advice and real concern that deep in our hearts we know is sincere and God-sent.

Sometimes these God-sent people tell us things about our children that we do not want to believe and so we turn a blind eye because it's easy. They may point out a flaw in our parenting, offering suggestions to deal with a situation; as our egos and pride become bruised, we sometimes attack the messenger (possibly God's messenger) and ignore the message, or we cut ties with them. At this point, discernment is key.

Pray when receiving the message—about you or your children—and while considering the messenger. Be open to what God reveals to you, even if it means eating humble pie. If God sends the message, with prayerful discernment, our hearts will know this; we need to thank messengers for loving us (and/or our children) enough to say and do the right thing to help us. Trust your gut and pray for wisdom. Listen with both your head and your heart. Though most messengers may be well-intentioned, not everyone is a godsend.

Real Life Village People: Bekie

Years ago, when my oldest daughter, Bekie was a junior in high school, her closest friend became pregnant. During a sleepover at our house, the friend tearfully revealed this to my daughter and me, producing two positive pregnancy tests taken earlier that day as evidence. After prayer and a long conversation, the friend decided to invite her mother to our house for the difficult conversation.

Throughout the discussion, the mother glared angrily at Bekie and me, as if we were responsible for her daughter's predicament. Then, without a word, she stormed out of my house with her daughter, slamming the door behind them.

Two weeks went by before Bekie's friend returned to school.

"I can't hang out with you," she informed my daughter.

"What? Why?!" Bekie responded, incredulously.

"My mom says you're a bad influence." With that, Bekie's friend walked away. The girl's mother followed up with a phone call to reiterate what her daughter had said.

"My daughter was not pregnant, and I don't appreciate you telling anyone she was!" (We had not shared this information with anyone.)

My daughter cried, blaming herself for trying to help. I had to remind her (and myself) that sometimes, even when we do the right thing, we are not well received by others; our help may be rejected.

Other times, we, too, blindly reject help from well-intentioned people, even when that help is God-sent. When you receive or give help to others, it's important to seek discernment and God's guidance.

Though sometimes rejected, we are still not excused from the village. We should continue to receive God's messengers and messages. We must be about the business of building our village. We need to put our pride aside, and let God guide; in His wisdom, He'll provide.

Bekie has since become a master at building her village. She is now a young mother with a wonderful husband and three children. She and her husband have shown great wisdom in choosing, building, and investing in their village. Most recently, when one of her friends lost her husband, my daughter and her friends (their village) came to the rescue, cooking meals, babysitting, and counseling with the children—even taking turns staying overnight several evenings until the young family's grief subsided and they were better able to cope with the loss.

My daughter's village invests in itself—its members care for, support, and encourage one another through the good and the bad. From babysitting, carpooling, and family get-togethers, to playdates and vacations, they share core values, provide love, demonstrate faith, and work to lighten the load of each villager. They truly epitomize the meaning of "village."

Look for opportunities to build and enlarge your village. Find those friends, teachers, coaches, leaders, and students who really care about your child. At church, which people (adults and peers) are sincerely connecting with your child? Which family members are invested? Which community members?

Welcome your children's input in this process, and really listen to their feedback. On most occasions, when it comes to determining the adults who really care about them, kids know. They feel it. They sense it. Just ask. Be sure to take the time to follow up by finding out as much as you can about these people to ensure their influence truly is a healthy one for your child.

If you determine that someone is not a good or healthy influence for your child, speak up. Be your child's advocate, no matter the person or situation. Pray for guidance and be strong, loving, firm, and calm in taking this stance. Do not let your emotions rule you in this process, as emotions often mislead us. They keep us from seeing all of the truth and/or lead us to doing the wrong things for the right reasons.

Do your homework, and learn as much as you can about the person and the situation(s) when taking action. Quiz your own child in this process, and leave no stone unturned. Be prepared to administer direction, knowing that you may have to keep your child from hanging out with particular "friends" and/or people. Such supervision may cause your child to feel angry or resentful toward you, but it's a warranted safeguard.

Village People

Remember—be the parent during the growing-up years. Your children need your parental guidance more than they need your friendship.

On the other hand, consider the individuals in your child's village who have a positive influence. How are you investing in them? How are you teaching your children to invest in, and give back to, others? This can be just as important as choosing your village because in this process, you teach your children the importance of giving as well as receiving. You are developing the spiritual and emotional character that God wants your children to have.

Let me share a quick story about how I chose my village during a rough time in my life. I was a divorced, single parent raising three children on a teacher's salary. Needless to say, we were scrimping to make ends meet.

We were friends with two wonderful, Christian families, the Lehmans and the Kings, who supported and encouraged my children and me in many ways. One evening, when we were all having dinner at my house (my way of investing in them), my younger daughter, Cali, innocently stated to our company, "I knew we were having company for dinner because Mom always makes spaghetti when we have company."

"Oh," Doris responded. "Is that your mom's favorite meal?"

"No," Cali chuckled. "Mom says it's cheap to make, it goes a long way, and we can eat it as leftovers all week since she's saving up to buy a bed 'cause her back hurts from sleeping on the floor."

Humiliated, I quickly laughed and changed the subject, offering homemade cookies as dessert. The next evening, there was a knock at my door. My friends, Sally and Doris, greeted me and brought in four bags of groceries. Their husbands pushed past me, with mattresses and a bed frame in tow.

"My grandmother passed away a few months ago, and we've had this bed just sitting in our garage, collecting dust. It needed a good home," Sally explained.

As I started to protest, Doris began to put groceries in my cabinets and refrigerator. "As we've been blessed, we are to bless others," she stated. "So, don't deny us this blessing." As I brushed away tears, I was suddenly surrounded with hugs from my village people.

I'm not sure how well my children or I would have survived my divorce without the help of our village. From fun moments such as Motown, wooden-spoon sing-offs, camping at Greenleaf State Park, and late night suppers with heart-to-heart conversations, our supporters provided love, joy, laughter, and encouragement to get us through this challenging time.

They babysat and mentored my children. They shared uplifting quotes and scripture with me. They cooked dinner and invited us to spend quality time with them. They checked in on us regularly. And, when I quit attending my church because I felt ostracized and outcast as a divorcee, my friends and family invited me to theirs. They never gave up on me . . . or my children.

Village People

As stated earlier, parenting is hard work. We—parents and children—need all the help we can get. Who should be part of your village? Who are your village people?

Coaching Time

Invite your children to be part of this process and start with a prayer. Work together to choose your village. Use the graphic organizer provided—or create your own.

My Village	Children's Village	Support Needed	Investments

1. Under the columns, *My Village* and *Children's Village*, list names while considering these questions:

    - Who has your best interests at heart? Who has your children's best interests at heart?

    - Who has the ability to bring out the best in you as a parent and person? Who brings out the best in your children?

    - Who cares enough to be honest with you rather than just agreeing with you to maintain an unhealthy harmony?

2. Whom can you trust, and whom can you trust with your children?

    - How do these people encourage you? Your children?

3. List what help you and your children will need from the people selected as villagers (i.e. encouragement, mentoring, etc.).

4. Under the column, *Support Needed*, list what help you and your children will need from the people selected as villagers (i.e. encouragement, mentoring, etc.).

5. Under the column, *Investments*, list how you and your children can/will support and encourage the people selected as villagers (i.e. babysitting, cooking a meal, etc.).

6. Contact your villagers to request permission to include them in your village, explaining the purpose and process.

Post the list so it is visible for reference and reminders. You might even include a column to list phone numbers of your village people for your children's sake.

Prayer: *Our Father in Heaven, with the many decisions and responsibilities that rest upon my shoulders as a parent, I need your help. Sometimes I feel so overwhelmed, so tired, and alone. I wonder if anyone understands what I'm going through. Hear my heart and lift my spirit. Please place the right people in my life, as well as in my children's lives to help in this process. I need encouragement and support. Your word reminds me I am not expected to do this work alone. Help me to select wisely for my village. I realize you have placed many in my path from whom to choose:*

family, friends, teachers, church leaders, and others. As I build my village, help me to encourage others in return, to bless them with my gifts just as you continually bless me. In your name, I pray. Amen.

Poem: I wrote this during my years as a single parent. It was a reminder of three things. 1) I needed the love and support of my friends and family. 2) They needed my love and support, and 3) We all needed to care for and protect this precious gift we shared.

The Gift

My gift to you cannot be found on the rack of any exclusive shop.

Nor is it on the shelves of any discount store. You won't find it displayed in a jeweler's window, or pictured in the most popular catalogue.

The mere essence of it can shape a child, shatter a heart, or heal the soul. It outsparkles the most brilliant diamond. It is stronger than a ton of steel. Yet it is more fragile than an eggshell.

No amount of money can buy it and it can never be stolen. It can be given but never taken. It can be shared but never owned.

Though you may travel across the widest deserts or sail the deepest seas, you can not escape it. You may climb the steepest mountains or cross the valleys' bottom, but you can not elude it. It is a gift that will stay with you if cared for. It is not something to neglect, abuse or deny.

It is hard to capture and difficult to define. Some days, it may feel light and breezy; other times, heavy and laborious. If you hold it too tightly, you may smother it. If you don't carry it with you, it may wither.

No amount of power can resist it. No amount of wealth can secure it. And no amount of fame can provide it. Despite the commonality of its giver, it is the most rare, the most wonderful, the most precious, the most expensive, and the most lasting gift one could ever give: It is Love.

Chapter 3

∽

MASTER YOUR MONSTERS
(AND I DON'T MEAN THE KIDS!)

"Fathers, do not provoke your children to anger, but bring them up in the discipline and instruction of the Lord."

Ephesians 6:4 ESV

After nine years of a troubled marriage, I found myself single with three young mouths to feed and souls to nourish. It didn't help that I was unemployed with a house payment, bills, and empty cupboards. During this tough time, not only did my monsters surface, but, at one point, they threatened to consume me.

We all have them—those monsters that invite us to indulge in self-sabotoging behaviors. They hinder us from being our best. They wreak havoc in our lives by inhibiting us from interacting with our children (and others) in healthy and productive ways. We fight these beasts on a regular basis, especially during our most vulnerable moments; it's *very* easy to fall prey to them. They seem to creep into our souls, like dark clouds hovering above us ready to rain down and drown out our best intentions.

The key to slaying these monsters is starving them. Refuse to give into them, because each time we do, even at the slightest level, they demand more from us the next time. They make it easier to give in again and again until, before we know it, we are that monster.

Recognizing, naming, and acknowledging our monsters is the first step to overcoming them. And, though they may never permanently be put to rest (due to stress, frustration, aggravation, fatigue, disappointment, depression, etc.), God can and *will* help us to successfully deal with them, if we will but ask and follow His commands. In fact, it is when we abide by His wisdom rather than our own, that we invite His strength and power into our lives. We can do more than simply deal with our monsters; we can overcome them.

We may not always be able to control what's happening to us, but we can control how we respond. We can develop wisdom and new habits through God to build self-discipline and reliance on God.

James 1:5 tells us *"If any of you lacks wisdom, you should ask God, who gives generously to all without finding fault, and it will be given to you"* (NIV).

Peter writes, "*5 Make every effort to add to your faith goodness; and to goodness, knowledge; 6 and to knowledge, self-control; and to self-control, perseverance; and to perseverance, godliness; 7 and to godliness, mutual affection; and to mutual affection, love*" (2 Peter 1:5-7 NIV). In the end, doesn't it always come back to love?

God's word tells us we can master our monsters. Though it may be an ongoing battle, it becomes more manageable with practice and time, with habit. We must pray, look to our village, consider when professional help may be needed (according to individual situations), and, as I said, practice. It can be done.

My favorite support for this is found in Philippians 4:13, *"I can do all things through Him who strengthens me"* (ESV).

Henry Ford said, "Whether you think you can or think you can't, you're right." So believe, my friend. To master our monsters, we must develop spiritual strength, emotional muscle, and mental fortitude.

Think about it this way. If you were out of shape physically and started a new exercise program, you probably wouldn't start by running five miles, lifting weights, or stretching tight, unused muscles by doing the splits, would you? Building up that endurance, physical muscle, and flexibility would take time. It would be a process, and it would require continual workouts in order for you to stay in shape. The day you stop exercising those muscles is the day that you begin to lose those muscles.

Spiritual strength, emotional muscle, mental fortitude, self-discipline, and personal character require the same process. It is a moment-by-moment, conscientious effort that we must always attend to … a way of being, doing, responding. Our new choices become who we are. Our monsters are left behind.

This process will not be easy! In fact, this task may well be one of the toughest missions of your life, but, for me, it was a critically important one.

My monster is my anger, my temper. When I'm especially frustrated, this monster of mine seeps in quickly, working to possess me. I feed it by giving in to my emotions. I allow my feelings to rule my actions and my words. I succumb and let my heart override my head. My monster begins to speak and act for me. And each time I feed my monster, it grows.

With each ugly thought, each hateful word, and each selfish action, this monster snowballs into a dragon. There is no biting my tongue. There is no stopping to think. There is no prayer in my heart. There is no giving it to God.

Later, I realize that I did the opposite of what I intended. I spewed harsh, and horrible words. No amount of truth can excuse the fact that the way I spoke was damaging. My behavior was deplorable. If I saw myself on camera, I would be ashamed and embarrassed by the shoddy example I'd set for my children. I fed my monster. And that monster grew and grew and grew until it consumed me; it became me.

I especially remember one particular time that I refer to as my "monster moment." I had quit my job a year before in an attempt to salvage a crumbling marriage. As a single mom with three children, a hefty house payment, bills piling up, and no income, I was tired, scared, stressed, worried, frustrated, lonely, and angry. To top it off, I couldn't get credit, as all loans, etc. were in my ex-husband's name. I allowed those circumstances to justify my behavior.

One evening, I came home emotionally spent from several job interviews that hadn't panned out. Walking into the house, my kids trailed behind arguing about something silly. "Stop it!" I yelled. "I'm sick of hearing you argue! Go clean your rooms and bring your dirty clothes to the laundry room." I just wanted them out of my way for a few minutes.

As I scoured the cabinets for something to cook for supper, I only found tomato sauce, spaghetti, Ramen noodles, peanut butter, two cans of corn, and a bag of beans. That would feed us for a few days. But what about next week? That's all we had to feed my family of four.

I stood in the middle of the kitchen, staring at that can of tomato sauce, hypnotized by the worst-case scenario. I'm sad to say, I didn't pray. I didn't give it to God. I didn't practice what I had been preaching all these years; patience, kindness, courage, faith, trust, and the golden rule were nowhere to be found. Instead, I gave in to my emotions and exploded as I heard the kids arguing *again*.

Going from room to room, I shrieked like a crazy woman, picking up toys and clothing that hadn't been put away and throwing them across the room. "Is this where these shorts go? On the floor? You call this clean? Where do these toys go? What about these dirty dishes? I told you not to eat in your bedrooms. You don't appreciate anything!"

My kids scurried about, trying hard to please me as they attempted to explain themselves and pick up their rooms. I wouldn't hear it. I had begun to feed the monster inside me, and the monster was gaining strength.

"Don't you talk back to me, young lady. Watch your smart mouth or you'll get a swat on those sassy britches. Get back to work and shut your mouth!" At their hesitation, I shouted, "Now!" I turned to leave, stomping my feet.

As Jeremy carried the hamper to the laundry room, Bekie ran at him, jerking the basket to pull out her shorts. "You idiot—I told you these were clean!" she screamed at him.

"Well, stupid, you shouldn't have put them on the floor then!" He shouted back, shoving her. Their voices sounded just like mine, harsh and mean, as they participated in a tug-of-war with the hamper full of dirty clothes.

Without thinking, I grabbed the car keys off the cabinet and threw them at the washer next to where they stood. The keys clanged and jangled as they hit the metal before landing on the ground with a thud. My kids stared at me in disbelief, faces white with fear, eyes brimming with tears, and lips trembling to gain control. "You tried to hit us," Bekie accused, her voice breaking.

"No, my dear, I didn't. My aim is much better than that. If I'd tried to hit you, I would have," I said, glaring at the two of them. Surprised by my own actions, the monster inside (having been fed) became more subdued, leaving me to recognize my violent gesture. I shook my head. I had wanted to get their attention and I did. But, at what cost? They believed I was trying to hurt them, to hit them with a set of keys.

Tired and defeated, I shrugged. "Please, please, please, just go to your rooms. Clean them up. Stop arguing," I whispered, slumping to the kitchen floor.

Dinner was quiet. The kids went to bed early, probably out of fear rather than fatigue. I used that alone time to call my older sister and confess my sins.

She listened, provided suggestions, and kindly offered, "You're just under a lot of stress, Pammy. Don't be so hard on yourself. Your kids know you love them."

"Do they?" I wondered as Ephesians 6:4 popped into my head. *"Fathers [mothers, too], do not provoke your children to anger, but bring them up in the discipline and instruction of the Lord"* (ESV). Despite my sister's understanding, we both knew this was not my finest hour.

That night beside my bed, I literally fell to my knees. The guilt was all consuming. I wept silently, asking God for forgiveness, patience, self-control, and kindness. I prayed for strength to be a better example. I prayed for God to give me guidance and courage, to show me how to trust Him and put His will first. My kids deserved so much better, and I vowed to give them that—despite my stress, hurt and frustrations.

That was over twenty-five years ago. I'd love to say that monster is dead, but, occasionally, if I'm not careful, that monster comes roaring out again. The difference now is I remember to turn that monster over to God. I refuse to feed it. I stop to pray, think, and breathe before responding. When I'm feeling weak, tired, or I am about to sell out to my emotions, I allow God to step in and guide me. So, more times than not, love wins out, and the monster slinks quietly back into the night.

I'm sure you have "monster moments," too. The key is not to let those moments become a way of life.

Karen Wolff (*Raising Kids God's Way: Passing on Your Faith to Your Children*), warns that kids today "face an overall absence of godly examples and moral living in a society that is moving toward 'freedom from religion' instead of 'freedom of religion.' " If we don't consistently model God first for our children, who will?

Think about ways to master your monsters for the sake of your children. What are your habits and words? What are your ways of being with your children? Do you live in a way that would make them proud to call you Mom or Dad?

Where are you now? Where would you like to be? Consider ways that you might get there. It won't be an overnight transition; it'll be one thought, one deed, and one choice at a time. Commit to making the changes, and pray. Believe that God can help, and know that the monster will work harder than ever to keep you from those changes. Just remember, despite the frustrations facing you, you'll find help in your village of support. Look to God for a better way to handle life. Take a deep breath, whisper that prayer, and refuse to feed the monster.

Coaching Time

It's time for prayer, reflection, paper and pencil. Read the questions and respond honestly. Not intendend for judgment, these questions are meant to allow you to determine where you are currently, where you want to be, and how you can develop those habits and behaviors to replace any monsters influencing your parenting in a negative way. Put your goals in a visible place so that you can measure and monitor progress.

1. What monster(s) inhibit your parenting?

2. What changes, as far as word choices, behaviors, and habits, would you like to develop to starve that monster?

3. How will you be accountable for these changes and what evidence will serve as progress for you?

4. Look at the names of villagers listed in the previous chapter. Which people can help you in this process? Ask for their support.

Prayer: *God, help me to recognize, acknowledge, and understand the monsters in my life that keep me from being my best, both as a parent and as a person. Sometimes these monsters creep up when I least expect it, when the world around me is chaotic and seems out of control. Give me strength. Though I may not be able to control what's happening to me, I know that with your help, I can control how I respond. No excuses! Through you, all things are possible. Help me rely on you. Help me seek out the people and support needed as I master these monsters. Guide me in my efforts. Provide the encouragement and motivation to keep me diligent and faithful to your word as I develop parental habits that glorify you. In your name, I pray. Amen.*

Poem: Following is a poem I wrote while a single parent. Each morning I arose with a new determination to be patient and loving with my children. But as the day wore on and demands brought fatigue and frustration, my resolve often withered away much to my dismay. I continued to make that promise, however, and each day grew better with practice.

Night's Song

I tuck my babies in and smile down at droopy eyes, tousled heads, and rosy cheeks. As their childish clumsiness and curiosity is replaced with a sweet and precious innocence that radiates in the semidarkness, I vow to be more patient over spilled milk and crayon-colored walls; to discipline with a calm voice rather than in harsh tones, and to put away my books, studies, and outside interests to listen more intently to their childish chatter and participate in their games of make-believe and hide-and-seek.

Yet, as the sun brings a new day, my promises vanish when innocence is replaced with youthful mischief and exploration. Fatigue, demands, and impatience take over before night envelops the sky once more. Folding children like burritos into blankets, my lips kiss their foreheads. With heavy eyes, my babies resist the tug of slumber. As their warm breath brushes my face, I hear whispered sighs, "Love you, Mom." My throat catches as I stifle a sob. Gently closing their bedroom doors, I renew my vows, wondering why angels only come during the lullabies of night's song.

Chapter 4

∽

Let There BE ... Boundaries and Expectations

"The rod and reproof give wisdom, but a child left to himself brings shame to his mother."

Proverbs 29:15 ESV

"Discipline your son, and he will give you rest; he will give delight to your heart."

Proverbs 29:17 ESV

Consider the rod mentioned in the above scripture. It is not necessarily an instrument used to strike another person, but symbolizes a tool to guide, as in the twenty-third Psalm, *"Thy rod and thy staff, they comfort me."* In biblical times, shepherds used the crook in the staff to gently guide and move sheep back to the fold, keeping the sheep from harm. You can see how this might be a metaphor for disciplining children with love and direction.

Growing up as a child of the 70s, I recall a popular Beatles song titled, "Let It Be." The lyrics, written by Paul McCartney and John

Lennon, were reportedly inspired by a dream about Paul's mother, who died when he was only fourteen years old. In the dream, Paul, experiencing a troubled time, felt his mother attempt to comfort him by saying, "It will all be fine. Just let it be."

What is great about Paul's experience is that he still felt the comfort and influence of his mother so many years later. Though I doubt if even the greatest parenting could totally eliminate all struggles with our children, I firmly believe that sharing our wisdom in the form of boundaries and expectations will lessen the enormity and number of challenges. That's why I put a little twist on the title and say, Let *There* BE ... Boundaries and Expectations, that is.

Boundaries and expectations naturally lead to discipline and consequences. All are vital to helping children grow into caring, respectful, responsible, capable adults. They allow our children to learn how to handle life's challenges, to dance in the rain until the flowers grow, to be more determined and to become victors rather than victims.

There is a great belief in our society that children misbehave because they lack self-esteem. Perhaps it's more accurate to say children act up when they lack self-control. Thus teaching them self-discipline is critical.

As a former teacher and principal at the elementary, middle, and high school levels, I've worked with children most of my life. My purpose has always been to help children grow. To empower them. To grow their capacity as well as their gifts and talents. To help them know and see their own potential and self-worth. After all, that's what boundaries and expectations do. They save us from ourselves, while keeping us from infringing on the safety and rights of others.

Let There BE (Boundaries and Expectations)

My friend and former colleague, Maudye Winget, referred to this necessary balance as a conundrum, stating "Boundaries are the things that hold you in while expectations are what set you free." And we need both!

Speaking of expectations, Luke 12:48, says, " ... *From everyone who has been given much, much will be demanded; and from the one who has been entrusted with much, much more will be asked"* (NIV).

This scripture reminds me of my middle son, Archie ... not only my expectations for him, but also his expectations for himself and how these expectations helped him make his dream come true. From the age of four, it was obvious Archie had an extraordinary talent. He begged to play any sport involving a ball. Succumbing, we allowed him to play baseball, where he turned his first big play. After catching a pop fly, Archie threw the ball to first base (prompted by his coach), and the one-hopper worked to get a double play. The crowd went wild, and Archie was hooked. He loved the cheering, he loved the challenge, and, after that, he loved the game of baseball.

Archie quickly learned that though God blessed him with a tremendous gift, it was Archie himself who needed to develop that talent, or let it be wasted. While summer saw most kids swing from trees, Archie swung his bat. While his friends ran races, Archie ran bases. As his buddies practiced stunts on bicycles, Archie practiced his curveball. While others perfected their video games, Archie was perfecting his game.

Despite the fact that he demonstrated both a love and dedication for baseball, we still had a duty as parents to encourage, support, and sometimes goad Archie in his pursuit. For him to play competitive baseball, he had to help earn the money to attend those camps. He spent summers traveling with his team, as this was necessary for furthering his dream. He also understood that practice was mandatory for him, not something he could choose whether or not to attend. Finally, he understood that if we, as parents, were investing this much of our time, money, and energy, he would need to do the same; there would be no sloughing off. After all, developing his character as a person was just as important as developing his skills as an athlete.

One game, he jogged to get a poorly thrown ball, costing his team a run. What bothered me wasn't that he missed it, but rather his lack of effort. After the game, I addressed it.

"Arch, what was the deal out there? You didn't make much of an effort to get that ball in the last inning."

"It was hot, I was tired, and, besides, that kid made a bad throw," he responded.

"Was that fair to your team?"

"No," he muttered, "But … "

"Here's the deal," I interrupted. "If you want to play recreation ball, that's fine. You can do that and we'll just play league in Muskogee. However, if you want to play competitively and travel from state to state, I'd better see you hustling at all times and giving it your best. I'm not spending my whole summer and all this money to watch you slough off. If you're not serious about this game, let's quit wasting your time and mine. So what's it going to be? Rec ball or competitive? You decide."

That was all I had to say. Archie knew our expectations for him. And, he had expectations for himself, learning that his investment to this sport mattered more than ours. As a result of his self-discipline and commitment, Archie was signed (right out of high school) by the Arizona Diamondbacks as the seventh overall first-round pick in the 2011 MLB draft. Still, his expectations for himself—along with hard work and commitment—are necessary for him to progress.

Expectations and boundaries matter. Some children wander through life trying to figure out what's wrong and what's right, what's good and what's bad, what direction they should take, and which pathways they should avoid. While some exploration is good for children, too much with too little guidance can be disastrous.

While most kids desire freedom, often unbeknownst to them, they are also crying out for boundaries. They want someone to have expectations for them. They want limitations. They want someone to consider what's best for them and to provide guidance along the way. They want parents to care enough to say no. Yet, too many parents are afraid to do just that.

"It makes me feel mean," one mom told me.

"It prevents my daughter from exploring who she wants to become," another said.

"It's too limiting."

"I don't want my kids to hate me."

"My parents were too strict on me so I vowed I'd let my child do what he wanted."

"Oh, they'll figure it all out when they grow up."

And the misguided reasoning goes on and on. Statements from parents who are too afraid to be, well ... a parent. Worrying too much about being "liked" by their child. Not wanting to be considered "uncool" by their children's friends. Not liking the idea of being the "bad guy" when it's time to firmly say, "No."

Yet, we are told in Isaiah 54:13, *"All your children shall be taught by the LORD, and great shall be the peace of your children"* (ESV).

And in 2 Timothy 3:16-17, *"16 All Scripture is breathed out by God and profitable for teaching, for reproof, for correction, and for training in righteousness, 17 that the man of God may be competent, equipped for every good work"* (ESV).

As parents, we want our children to grow into caring, responsible, resourceful adults. We want them to be problem solvers, evolving into creative, self-sufficient people, able to survive and thrive in the world around them. Yet, in reality, it's hard for us to let go and let them grow because we want our children to "need" us.

Because of this need to be needed, we often cross the line from support to enabling, creating instead a sense of entitlement in our children. It's a battle that must be faced and acknowledged in order for us to get it right.

So, how can we as parents empower our children, rather than enable them, or worse, cause them to feel entitled to things in life for which they have neither worked for nor earned? It's a tough and delicate balance, but it's one of vital importance.

Let There BE (Boundaries and Expectations)

We help our children experience significance when we expect them to contribute to the greater good of others. It is in giving and acting unselfishly that they will find a sense of purpose and belonging.

Here are some tough questions I had to grapple with throughout my thirty-seven years of foundational parenting: How are my children contributing to our family? What required chores do they have? Have I taught and modeled for them how to do those chores, or do I just do it for them because it's easier and faster? Should I pay them for all the chores they do, or should they be expected to do some of those chores without pay as their contribution to our family?

If I give my children everything their hearts desire, how is that developing in them a sense of value? A strong work ethic? A need to contribute and give back? Will they really learn to appreciate, or will they just expect more?

I had to decipher my children's needs from their wants, and the necessities I should provide them versus what they should earn. Boundaries and expectations helped me figure it out.

We, as parents must provide a consistent structure for our children that allows them to be safe, teaches them to be considerate of others, and reminds them that they, too, have a responsibility to contribute and to make the right choices. Then, based on their choices and actions, allow them to live and learn from the consequences that follow, whether those consequences are natural and/or parent provided.

When it comes to discipline and consequences, we can all learn a lesson from Dr. Seuss's, *Horton Hatches an Egg*. In the book, Horton says over and over, "I meant what I said and said what I meant. An elephant's faithful one hundred percent." Horton then matches his words with actions. As parents, we, too, need to mean what we say and say what we mean, and then match that up with corresponding actions ... something I had to learn to do.

Years ago, while shopping with a friend, my two young children, Jeremy and Bekie, began throwing a tantrum after I refused to buy them candy. Jeremy screamed at the top of his lungs while Bekie threw things out of my cart. As a young mother, I wasn't quite sure how to handle such behavior. Exasperated, I whispered, grabbing each by the arm, "I'm going to count to three, and if you don't stop, I'm going to give you both something to cry about!" I counted out loud, deliberately and firmly emphasizing each number. "One ... two ..." I paused as my children carried on.

A lady in the aisle gasped when she passed me, rolling her eyes at my threat. An older gentleman shook his head, frowned at me, and muttered under his breath for me to "get those brats under control." Even my friend seemed annoyed.

I counted again, but neither of my children responded. On and on it went. I counted, and they ignored me. "One, two, three! Did you hear me? You're going to get your little hineys swatted if you don't listen!"

Five minutes later, exhausted and exasperated, I finally made good on my threat. Both kids began to wail loudly, and I panicked, quickly handing them a lollipop from the checkout counter just to shut them up.

Let There BE (Boundaries and Expectations)

As I loaded kids into the car, my friend turned to me, and in a patronizing voice, muttered, "You know what you just did, don't you?"

I shook my head, puzzled.

"You just taught your children they can do what they want on counts one and two. They don't have to mind until you get to the count of three. Then, you gave into them. They got what they wanted. You showed them their temper tantrums worked. Sheesh, Pam! Quit counting, and just take action! Don't say it unless you mean it!"

I glared at her, too stunned and hurt to respond. Later, however, as I reflected on what she was saying, I realized she was right.

From that day forward, I vowed to do just that, just as Horton did. "Mean what I say and say what I mean." changed the way I disciplined. I gave my children consequences that made sense for bad behavior, and I explained and communicated my boundaries and expectations to my children. No more counting over and over. I meant what I said the first time. No more waiting to take action, especially once I had given my children an appropriate explanation. No more disrespect or disobedience from them without consequences.

Speaking of consequences, this was another learning curve for me. I had to learn how to provide suitable consequences, taking into account the actual deed as well as each of my children's different personalities, and then determining what made sense for each child. Sometimes I allow the natural consequence to serve, like the time my seven-year-old son ran into the bushes to knock down a hornets' nest after being told to steer clear of that area many times. Unfortunately, he was stung above the eye not once, but twice. Of course, no other consequences were necessary.

Or the time one of my children stole something from the mall. That required a parent-given consequence, one that would teach a lesson about character and life. On a dare, my seventh-grade son stole a bottle of cologne from a department store and a friend reported the incident to me. My heart fell to the floor. I was embarrassed. I was mortified. And for a while, I made the focus about me, not my child. I worried about what people would think of me as a principal, as a parent, and as a member of the community. How could my child do such a thing to me?

Then I realized this was not about me as a parent. After all, my husband and I had long ago established expectations for our children to do the right thing in all situations, even under strong peer pressure. We taught them that stealing was wrong, and that if you wanted something in this life, you were to work to earn it. We taught it. We modeled it. We served as an example for this.

Therefore, I realized the focus was not about us as parents. I had to put everything in perspective before I could respond. I couldn't feed the monster threatening to overtake my whole being. This was about my child, his choices, and his actions. I took a deep breath, said a prayer for guidance, and knew that my husband and I had a very difficult decision to make. This was a time for cool heads to prevail and for boundaries and expectations to be firmly reestablished.

Interviewing my child, I quickly received a full-blown, snot-hurling, tear-soaked, remorseful-because-he-knew-it-was-wrong-and-sorry-he-got-caught-and-he-knew-he-was-in-big-trouble confession. I don't know who was more mortified when we entered that store—my son, or my husband and me. Nervous the store might take legal action, we took our chances, knowing this was the right thing to do. For a moment, I wanted to just ground my child, take away the cologne, and return it to the store with as little fanfare as possible.

I prayed for a different response, but God's answer was the same. My heart ached for my child, and my gut twisted, but I knew it had to be done. My son had to face the music and make this right, and we had to be there with him, in support of doing what was right.

After explaining his poor choice to the store clerk, my son handed the cologne back, along with forty dollars of his allowance. "But, it only cost twenty dollars," the clerk stated, trying to hand back the other bill, along with the cologne.

"Nope. I have to pay double and I can't keep the cologne." Looking at me for approval, my son added, "You can donate this to a charity. I'm sorry for stealing." He hung his head and stifled an embarrassed sob before continuing, "It won't happen again."

Back in the car, my son cried again, this time with more remorse. "I'm so sorry for what I did. I don't know why I did it. I thought it would be funny." I heard snot being sucked back into his nostrils and realized he was doing all he could to hold it together. "It was really stupid, and I promise I'll never do anything like that again."

The embarrassment and disappointment inside of me melted away. Instead, I felt only forgiveness, compassion, and a deep love for my son. I reached back and pulled his sweaty, neck toward me, kissing his tear-soaked cheek as I leaned over the seat. "I'm proud of you. I know that wasn't easy having to face the music and own your actions, but it was necessary," I said. "I love you more than life itself."

As he continued to sniffle quietly on the long ride home, I wanted to hold my son's skinny frame in my arms and rock him until all the pain in his little heart was gone. However, I knew those emotions were needed for the lesson learned. I knew the actions taken by my husband and me were required for the character-building process. I knew my son had to experience the humiliation, regret, remorse, and then accountability for his choice, in order to influence his future behavior. Despite our son's bad decision, we all scored a victory because of the life lesson learned. I realized that love is often best demonstrated through necessary boundaries.

Unfortunately, as a principal and parent, I've seen, heard, and experienced scenarios where children grow up with too few boundaries. A child-turned-adult too early makes unwise choices or acts irresponsibly without intervention or guidance, thus resulting in one or more of many sad scenarios: broken relationships, inability to keep a job, jail or prison time, and financial and/or emotional struggles. How will parents handle it when the child turns to them with tears, anger, and blame asking, "Why didn't you stop me? Why didn't you tell me this would happen? Why did you let me do something so foolish? Didn't you care?"

When a child makes a mistake, ask if you're making the situation about yourself. If so, refocus. Take time to cool off and pray before responding. Ask for God's guidance and search the scriptures. Although a consequence may be necessary for instructive purposes, it should be done in love and in a constructive way meant to change and build, not demean or force. Consider whether you are responding with judgment, resentment, anger, and punishment, or with love, wisdom, guidance, and mercy. Rather than belittling, determine how you can build character. Verify what really happened and whom your response was about.

I'd rather deal with the world's wrath than God's disappointment in me. I think about that when I'm reluctant to administer loving discipline. That allows me to determine what my response as a parent will be. If you care about your children, love them enough to discipline them. Provide boundaries and expectations. Let there BE and don't wait!

Coaching Time

Time to pray after grabbing paper and pen. It's coaching time!

1. What boundaries and expectations do you currently have for your children?

2. How can you provide boundaries, expectations, discipline, and consequences in a structure that:

    - Keeps your children and others safe?

    - Builds your children's character?

    - Helps your children to grow to be accountable, responsible, and pleasant individuals?

3. Prepare in advance for those times when your child will make mistakes and choices that may be embarrassing to you. How can you keep the focus on what's best (in a constructive way) for your child, rather than responding in a way that makes the scenario about you?

Prayer: *Lord, I come asking for your wisdom and guidance in this difficult, but rewarding journey. Help me as a parent to respond to my child with love, mercy, and forgiveness. Keep judgment, resentment, and self-focus from my heart and allow my actions to be a reflection of you. Be in my mind and in my heart as I establish boundaries and expectations for my child. Provide me with courage and understanding to determine the most appropriate consequences so my child may learn and grow for your purposes. In your name, I pray. Amen.*

Poem: Following is a poem written by me as a teenager. Its purpose was to keep me mindful of the importance of boundaries ... of seeking out wise counsel ... God's way during life's struggles.

Let There BE (Boundaries and Expectations)

A Better Way

You try to hide
The fear inside
The misery and tears you've cried,

You're searching for,
A little more
Than what life seems to have in store,

With little hope,
You try to cope,
And hold on to life's desperate rope,

Confused and lost,
Is what it cost,
To let desire be your boss,

Life's done you wrong,
Your strength is gone,
The road ahead looks hard and long,

Pick up your heart,
Don't fall apart,
Right now's the time to make your start,

Don't run away,
From life today,
Through God there is a better way.

Chapter 5

Making Moments to Remember

"This is the day that the Lord has made. We will be glad and rejoice in it."

Psalm 118:24 NLT

For parents, there is no greater compliment than when an adult child returns home to spend holidays or special time with you by choice rather than responsibility. Remember this during the growing-up years with your little ones, because if you don't make time for them now, you can probably bet they won't make time for you once they are grown.

Consider the time you currently spend together and what family activities, events, and trips your children may fondly recall. How are you creating memories that make them want to return home (without being overindulgent, enabling, or financially supporting them beyond childhood)?

That our example influences our children is a given. Our guidance leaves an imprint upon their lives. Therefore, let's make sure that when our children are grown and only memories of us are left, they recall them with joy and thanksgiving.

Lee Ann Womack's beautiful recording, "I Hope You Dance," captures the essence of how such impressions may impact our children. The lyrics embody a balance so many of us strive to provide our children: experience and fully appreciate life; to be neither grudging or greedy; to give and not just take; appreciate rather than presume; and be present for the joy, beauty, and opportunities God has provided. The song is so powerful, I dedicated it to my children (download it to understand what I mean). To me, it's a reminder to make memories that will touch my children's hearts long after I am gone.

Life is a gift, and children are a blessing. Making the right choices, demonstrating righteousness, and choosing to be involved in our children's lives enriches not only us, but our children. We must choose to be active participants in our children's lives. We must be present, and we must serve as Christian role models for them.

Some of my best times with my children never cost me a dime, just my time. In fact, I found a way to make even our most dreaded task, housecleaning, somewhat fun. My three older kids laughingly cite the times we'd crank up Motown and dance throughout the house playfully popping dishtowels in the air, or twisting our hips using the mop or broom as a partner. We'd bop down the hall belting out the lyrics to "Ain't No Mountain High Enough," "Proud Mary," or Leslie Gore's "It's My Party." To this day, every time my children hear certain songs, they point to me and start singing, reminding me of the fun we had together.

Deuteronomy 6:6-9 tells us: "*6 These commandments that I give you today are to be on your hearts. 7 Impress them on your children. Talk about them when you sit at home and when you walk along the road, when you lie down, and when you get up. 8 Tie them as symbols on your hands and bind them on your foreheads. 9 Write them on the doorframes of your houses and on your gates*" (NIV).

To do this, we must invest in our children, in their well-being and in their upbringing. We must invest our time, and a lot of it! That's not to say our children should always have our undivided attention. Not only is that unrealistic, it's unhealthy and may lead to our children feeling entitled, and resulting in an inability to entertain themselves.

My point is this. We often make the mistake of promising time to our children and then allowing our physical presence to be enough. It's not. When we set aside such time, we must commit to being emotionally, mentally, physically and spiritually available. We must choose to be in the moment fully ... not in our cell phone, not in our laptop, not in our iPad, and not in the television.

JEREMY

I remember when my son, Jeremy, was ten years old. He could barely contain his enthusiasm as we prepared dinner one night together.

"I have a surprise for you, Mom!"

"So tell me," I prompted as we sat down to eat. My thoughts moved ahead to the mounds of laundry, papers to grade and my promise of "kid time" tonight. Fatigue began to set in.

"Nope," he chuckled, stuffing bread into his mouth. "You have to wait." Dinner was rushed and he and his sisters quickly cleaned the kitchen while I stole minutes for other work in the living room.

"Okay!" Jeremy declared, pulling a blue paper from his school folder. "The surprise!" By the excitement in his voice, I could tell he had something quite special to share. His big, hazel eyes lit up and his voice rose with excitement. Just as he handed the paper to me, the phone rang.

"Hang on," I said, handing the paper back as I moved to answer the phone. It was my friend, just calling to chat. Jeremy retreated to the piano, softly running his fingers over the keys while he waited. "I'll just be five minutes," I told him.

Fifteen minutes later, the music stopped as Jeremy stood. He pointed to the blue paper in his hand. Bekie flipped on the television and Cali plopped on the floor as it appeared game night was not going to happen any time soon. "Just a minute," I promised, signaling again to my three children.

Ten more minutes passed and Jeremy came into the kitchen, this time waving his blue paper. He rolled his eyes in exasperation as I held up a finger.

"But, Mom," he said.

I shook my head, pointing to the phone.

He pointed to the clock.

"Would you just be patient?" I whispered gruffly, holding my hand over the phone as I grew agitated with him.

Forty minutes later, I clapped my hands, indicating completion of the phone call. Cali was curled into a ball, sleeping soundly. Bekie was immersed in a television show and Jeremy sat sullenly on the couch, still holding the blue paper in his hand.

"Now, what were you trying to tell me?" I asked.

"Nothing, Mom. It doesn't matter now." Jeremy shoved the blue paper into his folder and stomped off to his room.

I shrugged it off, thinking he was acting like a spoiled brat. He'd share with me once he cooled off. I stooped to carry Cali to bed. Bekie headed to the shower and I was secretly relieved. I could now turn my attention to the demands that called me earlier.

Buried in paperwork with the sound of the washer spinning in the background, I heard the clock strike 10 pm. I rose from the table and walked into Jeremy's bedroom to say goodnight. Hearing my voice, he turned toward the wall and covered his head with a blanket.

"Really?" I muttered under my breath. Sitting on the edge of his bed, I heard a paper crunch under my foot. Looking down, I noticed the blue paper Jeremy had attempted to hand me. It was wadded into a tight ball on the floor. I picked it up and smoothed out the wrinkles.

Dear Parent(s),

Congratulations! Your child received a score of Outstanding during the district piano recital. Your presence is requested at the upcoming concert where he will be honored for this accomplishment.

I caught my breath as I realized what I had done, not just today but so many times before. I put my son on hold. I made him wait despite the commitment that tonight was our time. I took care of my business when I should have been attending to his.

"Jeremy! What an honor!" I exclaimed softly, waving the crumpled note.

He looked up, slanting his eyes as they adjusted to the light in the hall. "It doesn't matter," he told me, snuggling back into his blankets. His body language said it all. I had blown it. In essence, my earlier actions had communicated to him a different intent. His interpretation of my actions was: *I don't matter to you, Mom. Your words are empty promises.*

I hit the pause button with my son that night, and I never did get to rewind. What a sad lesson for me. That moment is gone forever.

I made a vow. In the future, I would make a concerted effort to be wholly present in promised time with my children. Convicted, I leaned over to hug and congratulate my little musician. I kissed his cheek, shared my pride in his accomplishment, and apologized for my actions earlier that day. In the kitchen, I placed the blue note on my refrigerator with a star magnet, thanking God for the valuable lesson learned. Then, I turned to the calendar and penciled in tomorrow's date as game night.

COMMUNICATION

Spending time means much more than being physically present. It also involves communication. As parents, we may think we have all the answers, great advice, and wonderful wisdom to impart to our children. We do all the talking and our children do all the listening. Kind of one-sided, don't you think?

Children want to be heard, seen, listened to and hugged *daily*. Not only do they want us to be present, but they want presence, which encompasses much. Presence means that in conversations, we invite two-way communication (and we do much of the listening). Presence means we are active participants in our children's interests, alert to what they're up to as well as who they're hanging with, at school and elsewhere. It means creating schedules that allow for meals together with the television off and our attention on. It means building a communication process meant to influence their lifetime.

THE IMPORTANCE OF TRADITIONS

One way to create special memories is through traditions. Humans love tradition! In fact, even babies appreciate everyday rituals. They want to know what to expect next, because such routines ground them and give them a sense of stability and comfort. As adults, we are much the same. We never outgrow the need for grounding and tradition.

From trimming the Christmas tree to serving red, heart-shaped pancakes on Valentine's Day, it's easy to provide special moments for our children. Even things as simple as Mom's homemade tacos for birthdays, forty-five minutes of playtime before homework, Dad reads one story every night before bed, or opening one present on Christmas Eve will allow children to acquire a slew of warm recollections.

Traditions not only help us create our family culture, they can be passed down for generations. These are the things that connect us and bring us back home both literally and figuratively. We as parents provide the cornerstone of family life around which memories are created.

Consider those traditions that your children, no matter what age, will find comforting. What quality time are you spending with them? What memories are you making? These questions stay at the forefront of my mind. My goal is to create the kind of memories my children will want to rewind over and over again in their minds, and most importantly in their hearts, for years to come.

Coaching Time

Grab paper and pencil to respond to these questions as you reflect and pray about time with your children.

1. How do you currently spend your time each day? What percentage is spent with your children? Work? Serving God? Other?

    You may wish to create a pie chart based on percentages to represent how you typically spend your time daily (shown here).

2. How will your children define your time together?

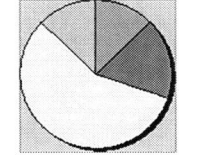

3. How do you define yourself as a role model for your children? How would they define you? What might they say about you when they are grown?

4. How will you create quality time for your children? List steps/changes you will make, being mindful of activities, playtime, conversations, scriptures, etc. to guide you. Remember, making memories with your child does not require money; it simply requires your time.

Prayer: *Father, you've blessed me with time and family. Help me to create special moments and traditions for my children that show my love for them. Give me energy to play when I'm exhausted. Despite the hectic demands of the world, remind me to schedule time for you, my children, and other family and friends. Allow me to point out to my children those silver linings when dark clouds hover above. Remind me to dance during the storms of life, demonstrating the importance of joy, faith, and a positive mindset in this world. Help me to make my time with family purposeful, fun and memorable in all the right ways. In your name, I pray. Amen.*

Poem: I wrote this from a child's perspective, recalling special moments and traditions shared with my sisters and family members. These memories keep home in my heart.

Remember

Remember those days of Hide-and-Seek, Mother-May-I and Red Rover? When we sang dolly lullabies and pushed make-believe carriages? Remember suppers at the round table and blanket-tents on the backyard clothes-line?

Remember comic book Saturdays, swimming pool tea parties, and homemade skits? Bobby-pin perms, pigtails and Shag haircuts? Remember climbing trees, tough-girl clubs and foot races against the neighborhood kids?

Remember when we put dreams into songs while riding in the back of Daddy's old, black pick-up truck with dust and hair flying in our faces? And what fun we had piling on each other to sled down our hill on the battered, red sled and inner tubes? Remember the supposed Wolfman and our weekend-long slumber parties?

Growing up may have meant outgrowing childish dreams but it never meant growing apart! Our hearts have kept us bound and though troubles, time, distance and differences may work to separate us, our memories and kinship will keep us ever close ... both as sisters and more importantly as friends!

Chapter 6

SHINING BEYOND THE DIAMOND

"God has given each of you a gift from His great variety of spiritual gifts. Use them well to serve one another."
1 Peter 4:10 NLT

"Every good gift and every perfect gift is from above …."
James 1:17 ESV

God gives each of us a gift. A way to glorify Him. A platform for praise. Our children are born with such gifts, and we, as parents, must be mindful not only how we encourage our children to develop them, but how we teach our children to use these gifts. It's vital that we teach our children to seek God's purpose for the gift as we help them to "grow" in its use for the good of others.

Too often, as parents of gifted children, we do one of three things: (1) we fail to foster the potential of their gifts; (2) we too aggressively push the development of their gifts (sometimes for the wrong purposes); or (3) we fail to develop their character, allowing for conceit, rather than confidence to be infused within their hearts.

None of those responses are healthy, so I offer another option. Parental direction. Instruct your children to know talents and gifts come from God. He expects those gifts to be used for a positive purpose through service, contributions and charity. As we foster our children's gifts, ensure they are grounded by teaching them that arrogance toward others is never okay. It's hurtful and disrespectful. Finally, provide children with parameters and then consequences for inappropriate use of the gifts. While such direction is needed, it's also necessary for all to know why the other three options are not healthy for anyone. Let's look more closely ...

FAILING TO FOSTER

Suppressing or failing to foster the growth of our child's gifts may damage confidence and inhibit life outcomes. Many children grow into insecure adults who never realize or reach their potential. Such insecurities can lead to failed relationships, lost job opportunities, substance abuse, and/or years of counseling.

One example might be a child who has great potential and a love of music. Yet, we, as parents, might refuse to allow the child to take lessons as it interferes with *our* schedule. Or, perhaps we refuse to lease/purchase the musical instrument needed for our child, claiming it's "not in the budget," when resources may be available elsewhere if we but seek them.

Another example might be that we neglect to recognize and articulate to our children the many ways they are special. We must encourage and celebrate our children's uniqueness rather than comparing them to siblings or friends. Such judgment or failure to acknowledge may inhibit our children's gifts.

I'll never forget when I unknowingly did this to my youngest son, Alex. It surfaced one evening as we decorated our Christmas tree. We'd recently moved to Broken Arrow, where Archie was considered Wonder Boy, the quarterback with a rocket arm and the pitcher to lead the baseball team to state. Alex, on the other hand, was an awkward eighth grader, still growing into his adolescent body and settling into his new environment. For him, it had been a difficult transition.

As we hung ornaments, I began sharing with Archie what I had read in the paper that day about his accomplishments on the field. He thanked me for the praise and then playfully began to harass and pinch his little brother.

Though usually quick to retaliate with his own witty remark, Alex was not having it tonight. "Stop it, Archie!" he bellowed. "You're just stupid, anyway. You think you're such a superstar, don't you?! Well, you're not that great!" Alex stormed out of the living room.

Archie shrugged his shoulders and looked to me, puzzled by his brother's anger. "Geez, Alex! What's your problem? I was just kidding!"

I shook my head at Archie, gave a firm shush, and then followed Alex into his bedroom, where he quickly began wiping away the tears streaming down his face.

Closing the door, I grabbed him, hugging his large, sobbing body. "Alex, what in the world is going on with you?" I asked.

"I can't do it anymore, Mom!" he cried.

"Can't do what?" I asked.

"I can't live up to what Archie does. I can't be Archie!" he muttered.

"No one wants you to be Archie. We want you to be you. One Archie is all I can handle. I don't need another one," I replied. "Just be you, sweet, wonderful Alex. No doubles of either," I said chuckling.

"But Archie is a great athlete, and he's always in the paper, and everyone talks about what a great star he is. You and Dad do, too," Alex cried.

"But you are a star too, Alex. You are special in your own ways. God has called you to a different purpose. Your gifts call for something else. You have a huge heart that touches others with kindness and understanding. You have such favor with God, and you influence others in so many positive ways. Don't doubt yourself or your purpose on this earth, Alex. God has big plans for you."

We talked for thirty minutes more before Alex finally let out a deep, ragged breath and smiled. With his thick, hairy arms, he squeezed me into a bear hug, so tight I could barely (or, should I say bearly) breathe.

"Thank you, Mom," he sighed with relief. He looked at me as if I had suddenly given him permission to just be himself—that wonderful, big-hearted, God-loving Alex … that big, burly teddy bear whom the whole world seemed to love, including, and especially, his brother, Archie.

Unfortunately, I had assumed that Alex had known it all along, but he didn't. That incident reminded me how important it is to foster my children's development, to demonstrate and articulate appreciation for each of their own unique gifts and personalities.

It's also essential to support our children's dreams … to support them in the development of their potential, even when it may mean sacrifice on our part. This brings to mind Archie and baseball. When he started playing on a team at age four, the team practiced only twice a week, and the league was only five to six weeks long. This wasn't too much of an inconvenience for us as a family, so all was good. We could still vacation and have time at our beloved cabin on weekends.

However, by the age of ten, Archie had won numerous awards as a die-hard athlete. The competitive teams sought him out to play during the summer, which meant most of his weekends and weeknights were committed to either practices or games. Because he loved the sport so much and demonstrated a dedication and desire to developing himself in this area, my husband and I found a way to make it happen.

This commitment was not specific to Archie, however. We made similar sacrifices for all five of our children. My husband and I often had to go in different directions to support the development of all of our children's gifts. We carpooled, shuffled schedules, and became creative in multitasking and delegating household chores between and among all our children. I often took my laptop to practices to complete work and jogged around the baseball field in lieu of working out at the gym. My husband started work earlier in the morning, so he could be available in the afternoon to shuttle one of our kids to an activity.

Not surprisingly, we seldom had time for social events. Many family members and friends criticized us for the sacrifices we made for our children, but to us, those sacrifices were worth it. We made it work, developing solid friendships between the parents on the ball team, and spending quality time as a family, developing our children's interests and life skills.

Throughout this process, our children learned they, too, had roles to play. Since we were investing our money, time, and energy in their interests, they had responsibilities, and sacrifices would be made on their end as well. Developing gifts meant hard work, giving their best efforts, and lots of practice time (when they'd prefer to be watching television or playing video games). It meant developing the type of character and attitude for others to follow. It meant acting in the right ways, remembering their gifts were from God, and that they were chosen to use such gifts for His purposes.

THE AGGRESSIVE PUSH

"Pride goes before destruction, a haughty spirit before a fall."
Proverbs 16:18 ESV

The other side of helping children to develop their gifts is showing them how to refine their character in the process. Too often, with success comes pride. As parents, it's easy to get caught up in the many achievements of our children in a way where we may behave as overbearing braggarts. Celebrating the success of our children with our children is one thing, and is important. However, allowing our children to think they are superior and above reproach and not subject to rules that guide civil interactions, is another. It is the latter behavior that can cause our children to go from confident to cocky, not a good attitude for anyone.

God provides us with friendly reminders of just that. It is never wise for anyone to become boastful, especially in a demeaning or hurtful way. When we arrogantly flaunt the success of our children, it may appear we are discounting others. When we haughtily praise our children, yet, fail to keep them grounded in Christian principles, we may plant in them a sense of entitlement along with an unchecked ego, which can easily result in selfish conceit. Finding a way to impart character and confidence rather than cockiness in our children is a delicate process, especially for those whose gifts cause them to shine especially bright.

Such is the case with Archie. Though I believe in my heart that all five of my children are specially gifted, the world and the media continually send reminders of just how special Archie is. Or, perhaps how scrutinized his every action is.

Archie's gift first surfaced at the age of two, when he could hit a golf ball across our field and smash baseballs off the tee. With a double play at age four, he continued to astound coaches and fans alike. At eleven years of age, he pitched a sixty mph fastball, and in high school, he led the Broken Arrow Tigers to the State Championship with fourteen strikeouts. Highly recruited by colleges across the nation, Archie decided to forgo college when drafted in the MLB.

I don't share this to be a braggart, but to demonstrate how hard Archie must work to stay grounded. With all of the accolades and the world telling him just how exceptional he is, it is important he never think of himself as an entitled "superstar." Because of his influence and visibility, he must be more mindful of his behavior, words, and choices. Little eyes are watching, and little feet are following. His example as a Christian role model is crucial.

An opportunity to reflect on this came when Archie's team was playing in a national qualifying tournament. He and his teammates watched the semi-final game, knowing they were to take on the winner of that game. The boys cheered for an exceptionally talented but rival Oklahoma team playing against a Texas team.

As the game grew close, the Texas batter on deck began to taunt the Oklahoma pitcher. Calling time, the Oklahoma coach ran to the mound, whispering a directive, after which the young hurler deliberately threw toward the player in the warm-up circle, smashing him in the back. The batter in the box looked puzzled, wondering why the pitch wasn't thrown to him, as his teammate crumpled to the ground in great pain. When the umpire ejected the pitcher, the Oklahoma team's parents shouted obscenities and jeered. In response, the young pitcher pumped his fist in the air in a celebratory motion as he left the field, causing his fans to go wild. The team's parents cheered evermore loudly to demonstrate their support of the young star's action.

To my surprise, the coach did nothing to subdue the disruptive crowd, but instead added to the mayhem. Allowed to stay on the field, his presence continued to send a sad, influential message to all spectators and, more devastatingly, his players: *We are superstars. We don't have to abide by other's rules. We will do whatever it takes to win.* The coach had the parents under his spell. They seemed to live vicariously through their children's victories, never considering the consequences of their actions.

Character vs. Conceit

"For by the grace given to me I say to everyone among you not to think of himself more highly than he ought to think, but to think with sober judgment, each according to the measure of faith that God has assigned."

Romans 12:3 ESV

Back to the ball field. Later that afternoon while at the concession stand, I overheard many parents discussing the game-changing play that allowed the Oklahoma team to advance. A few were still laughing about the coach's directive, and it saddened me to think they were encouraging their twelve-year-old sons to compromise character for a ball game. They didn't seem to have a clue. I wondered how many times I had been guilty of the same. My stomach turned at the thought.

I returned to the stands as our boys prepared for the championship game. Before the ump could yell, "Play ball!" one of the mothers from the rival team ran in front of our row of chairs. Attempting to incite our parents, her curly, blonde ponytail bounced up and down as she shook her fists in the air, while shouting rude and obscene things. Refusing to be baited, our team parents focused our energy on cheering for our boys. The game was intense and unfortunately, we lost. The blonde ponytail danced across our row again, laughing wickedly and singing, "We are the Champions."

I would be lying if I said I wasn't tempted to yank that blonde ponytail to the ground and shout out, "Your little darlings behaved like self-absorbed stars!" Yet, I knew that wouldn't resolve anything. So instead, I smiled through gritted teeth and offered a sarcastic, "Good luck! I'll be praying for you." I know. I shouldn't have. It lowered me to another level, but I just couldn't help myself. When she jerked around to offer more obscenities my way, I realized it was time to move to higher ground, so I did.

As I left the stands, the other team's coach flagged me down, waving frantically. "Hey, Mrs. Bradley, as you know, we are headed to nationals, and we'd really like to have your son Archie pitch for us."

For a moment, the prestige blinded me. It was quite an offer. We'd be traveling to play in Florida at the Disney Complex in a national tournament where this team was seeded number one. What fun! What exposure! What a proposition! What temptation! Archie stood beside me, hopeful, his competitive nature already envisioning a national trophy sitting on his shelf. The team's parents encircled us with incantations, patting Archie on the back. "Yeah! We need this guy! Go with us to Florida!"

And then, the spell broke when *that* mom stepped down from the bleachers in front of me. *That* blonde, ponytailed, devil reincarnate.

That lady who led the other parents in rude chants and cheers throughout the game against us. She helped me put things in perspective. I almost thanked her as I came to my senses. The horrific, unsportsmanlike conduct, the pitch directed to hit and hurt another player, the obscenities and taunts shouted at us throughout the game. I knew it was easy to be drawn into such an environment, and I wanted my son to have no part in it. I'd made that mistake before. "I'm sorry," I stated firmly, shaking the flattering fog from my head. "But we can't go with you to Florida."

The coach's jaw dropped and then he responded, "Don't you know what you're passing up?" I nodded and nudged Archie ahead of me before I could change my mind.

As I walked toward the parking lot, Archie fell in stride beside me. "Why, Mom?" he asked, ignoring the voices from the grumbling parents behind us.

"Because it's about more than just playing with a winning team," I explained. "It's about what that team represents; it's about what you represent. As a team member, you take on the team's reputation, and if not careful, its character," I stated.

"Yeah, but they have a reputation for winning!" He said.

"I realize that," I replied, placing my fold-up chair in the trunk of my car. "As your mom, it's my job to guard and guide your character as well as to control the environment and the people who influence it."

"Yeah, but I won't act like that," he responded.

"Probably not," I said, shaking my head and slamming the trunk emphatically. "Probably not."

Archie shrugged his shoulders, knowing this meant case closed. He climbed into the front seat, and I could tell by his body language that he was dreading the inevitable lecture coming. "I know, Mom," he started before I could even speak. "I know what you're going to say, and I get it."

"You do?" I asked incredulously.

"Yes," he replied. "I've heard it a thousand times. I am supposed to use my gifts for God's purposes. Never compromise character. Good sportsmanship matters. It's not okay to purposely hurt someone just to win a game. I get it."

I glanced his way sternly, wondering if he was being sassy. He responded by playfully pinching my knee before breaking into a big grin. "You do have to admit, though ..." he said, pausing with a laugh. "At least they recognize talent!" And with that, he pounded his chest confidently, and pushed his seat back for the long ride home.

I never regretted that decision, and time has proven that it didn't hurt Archie either. Through the ups and downs of his minor league baseball career, Archie's efforts and attitude paid off. He recently made his professional debut as a starting pitcher for the Arizona Diamondbacks, going six innings with only one hit against the LA Dodgers' three-time Cy Young Award winner, Clayton Kershaw, one of baseball's most accomplished pitchers!

Yet, despite being a baseball star, Archie was never exempt from our rules. His baseball status never entitled him to poor choices or condescending behavior. Apathy was not allowed, and respect for others was a must! He was subject to all the rules that guided our household. We loved him too much to allow him to be the exception, and he understood that (most of the time).

Once, a news reporter who arrived to interview Archie after the draft was surprised to find him taking out the garbage.

"You mean you have to do that?" he asked incredulously.

"Yep," Archie responded with a chuckle. "As well as the dishes, my bedroom, laundry, and the lawn. Want to help?"

Archie has dealt well with the many challenges that come as a result of his status. He works hard to present himself as a young man of faith, as a teammate, and as a dedicated athlete. Focused on his goals, he remains tenacious through life's lessons, and boldly takes in stride the unpredictable bumps inherent in the baseball life. As a reminder that God has called him to a higher purpose, with baseball as his platform, Archie had his favorite scripture inked under one rib, *"Trust in the Lord with all your heart and lean not on your own understanding; in all your ways acknowledge Him, and He will shall direct your path"* (Proverbs 3:5-6 New King James Version). Even as a mom, I couldn't be upset about such a tattoo!

Atop that rich, red pile of dirt, Archie has been taught to consider how his actions speak for his team, for himself, for his family, and, most importantly, for his God. Though human frailties often prevail, Archie is encouraged, as are all of our children, to continuously stay strong in God's presence and prepare for how richly He will bless such efforts.

As we consider our children's gifts, we must also be receptive to our children's wisdom about our gifts. Cali, my youngest daughter reminded me of that one evening as we visited and cooked dinner together. These are moments I cherish, as they are much too rare now that she has her own family.

After watching the news, I confided in her. "Perhaps I should be doing more for the Lord, considering all the chaos going on in the world ... the war, ISIS, the Ebola breakout ... I wonder if I should go abroad."

Cali, looked up at me, her big, brown eyes gleaming as she smiled confidently. Her words were wise beyond her years. "Mom, not everyone can be a missionary, or a soldier, or a doctor, but that doesn't mean that God isn't using your gifts to serve Him. Your influence with us as a mother, as well as with your students, teachers, and the people around you is enough. God needs workers everywhere."

Her words touched my heart, and I knew that they were God-sent. My daughter had become my teacher. She had used her gifts to remind me of mine. The ultimate message? Use your gifts to shine on and beyond your platform. For Archie, that's a diamond ... a baseball diamond, that is. What is your child's platform(s)? What are your gifts as a parent?

Coaching Time

1. What are your children's gifts?
2. How have/will you foster the growth of your children's gifts as well as their character?

3. How have/will you guide your children to be mindful of God's purpose for their gifts? To "shine beyond the diamond?"

Prayer: *God, help me to recognize and foster the gifts you've provided my children in a way that glorifies you and serves your purpose. Show me as a parent how to best use my own gifts for your purpose. Teach me to model for my children the many ways in which their talents can serve as a platform to spread your word and give you praise. Let not the conceit of such gifts or the lure of the world diminish our character or our devotion to you. In your name, I pray. Amen.*

Poem: The following poem is a dedication to each of my five children and their special gifts.

To My Five Blessings

How privileged I am to be your mother. Specifically capable and extraordinary, each of you brings a special dimension to my life. Thank you for enriching my world with your gifts.

Jeremy: You are my SILVER LINING. Not easily deterred despite difficulty, your creativity and resolve enable you to find the positive in each situation. Resilient and determined, you refuse to allow excuses, instead growing stronger through hardships. Your optimistic energy is infectious, and your laughter is buoyant. Your example of perseverance is not only admirable, it's one from which we all can grow.

Bekie: You are my RAINBOW. Colorful and enlightening, you inspire all to search for the "pot of gold," not only in life but from within. Just as the sun shines after every storm, you bring warmth and joy in the face of adversity, refusing to let life's rain dampen your spirits. Your spunky character serves as a reminder that rain is as essential as sun to grow, flourish, and blossom. Not limited to just one color, your actions encourage others to make the most of their abilities. You teach others to dance in the rain until the flowers grow.

Cali: You are SUNSHINE. Your unique perspective and individualism provide an emotional lift to those you love. Your beauty, loyalty, and quick wit endear you to so many. Though your temper flares promptly when provoked, you are quick to forgive. Like sunlight on a prism, your faith in God glimmers to warm and light the lives of others. Gifted in many ways, you glow brightly as you move toward God's purpose for you.

Archie: You are a STAR. A dazzling light in a night sky, you are like a magnet, drawing others to you. You are admired, respected, and often envied because of your incredible talent. Authentic and charismatic, you create your own trends. You exude confidence and optimism, not easily daunted by challenging circumstances. Whimsical, spontaneous, and playful, you illuminate the world around you. Adaptable and buoyant, your presence radiates warmth and irresistible fun.

Alex: You are the MOON. You shine with hope, providing light to a sometimes dark world. You are intuitive, introspective, and kind. Leading by example, your gentle but indomitable spirit recruits the best in others. Insightful and sensitive, yet strong in mind, heart, and deed, your actions encourage and inspire all around you. Charitable and judicious, you see beyond the world to what could and should be. You are the essence of goodness.

Chapter 7

BLENDED BLESSINGS

"To every thing there is a season, and a time to every purpose under the heaven: A time to be born, and a time to die; a time to plant, a time to reap that which is planted; A time to kill, and a time to heal; a time to break down, and a time to build up; A time to weep, and a time to laugh; a time to mourn, and a time to dance; A time to cast away stones, and a time to gather stones together; A time to embrace, and a time to refrain from embracing; A time to get, and a time to lose; a time to keep, and a time to cast away; A time to rend, and a time to sew; a time to keep silence, and a time to speak; A time to love, and a time to hate; a time of war, and a time of peace."

Ecclesiastes 3:1-8 NKJV

If you've parented children other than your own, or had your mate parent your children, you can see how these scriptures well describe the blending of a family. With over 50 percent of American households affected by divorce, a large majority of parents can relate to such difficulties, and I'm no exception.

Holding My Father's Hand: Faith-based Parenting

After my divorce, I felt like a failure. I experienced such anger, disappointment, and frustration at not making my marriage work. I was skeptical of marrying again and wondered if I'd be parenting solo for the rest of my life.

Still, having grown up watching the Brady Bunch, I clung to such romantic notions. A pretty lady with three children meets a handsome dad with three sons. They marry, the children instantly like each other. The children love their new stepparents, and they all live happily ever after. The End.

So, when God brought Charles into my life, my cynicism turned to hope. I fell in love fast and hard. I could picture us as the Bradley Bunch. In fact, I never knew I could love a man as much as I love him (and I thank God daily for bringing him into my life). Yet, the initial problem in the first few years of our marriage wasn't loving him, but rather getting my children to love him and integrate him into their lives.

Ironically, throughout this time, I prayed constantly for a good mate for me, but I neglected to pray for a strong father figure for my children. Call it ignorant, call it selfish, or call it oblivious; I just didn't think to pray that way.

While dating Charles, I wasn't sure if he was "family material." He was a confirmed bachelor, and frankly told me that he didn't know if he would ever marry, even though he loved me. He didn't want to be a dad, and his friends often referred to him as Charles "Goodtime" Bradley. He was always the life of the party. He made me laugh and he taught me to have fun at a time I really needed it.

But how much fun would it be bringing him into my home as my mate? As a second father to my children? My doubts outweighed my hope, and for a couple of years, I distanced him from my children. We all spent time together, but I was deliberate and selective in how we spent our time, ensuring my children didn't become too emotionally attached to him, as well as making sure he took no actions toward disciplining my children. Of course, this may have contributed to our difficulties later, when we eventually married.

After almost five years of dating, we finally said, "I do." Charles was already thirty-six years old and quite set in his ways. He had no real concept of parenting. Yet, he saw himself as "the great rescuer," swooping in to aid the damsel in distress and her three misfit children. Our new family was going to be another party. He was going to be the fun father, a best friend to the kids and the coolest guy ever! My children were going to be ecstatic at this new addition to the family, welcoming him with open arms. Not quite.

Charles had expected the old-fashioned *Father Knows Best* scenario: a perfect home, tidy and clean with supper on the table and all of us sitting around talking. As Charles shared funny stories, we would all listen attentively. The children would respond, "Yes, Sir," to his every request, and we would coexist happily as the new Brady Bunch. Not so.

Between my children's mistrust and resentment of Charles, the differences in parenting styles, and Charles's lack of parenting experience, our first two years were rocky. We were rarely on the same page when it came to discipline. Charles had expectations that I felt were often unrealistic and sometimes harsh. Therefore, I intervened, sometimes rightfully and sometimes wrongfully, to maintain peace.

This happened most often after my children returned from a weekend with their dad. Because their dad's rules were different than ours, it seemed that we had to become the "hammer," cracking down to enforce how we did things in our home. As a result, the kids often were resentful, responding, "But Charles is not our dad."

I wasn't sure how to resolve the mounting dissension between my children and Charles. I often flip-flopped, taking different sides at various times, playing both sides of the fence. I often informed him he just didn't understand my children. I even went so far as telling him I'd handle the situation, foolishly dismissing his authority in front of them. My actions affected not only the relationship between my children and Charles, but ours as well.

My intent to appease always failed miserably. The decisions I hoped would cause everyone to get along and accept their new role in our family resulted in growing resentment. The new Brady Bunch vision faded quickly; I realized this wasn't television, and we weren't the Brady Bunch. I could not rescript those parts that were unpleasant. This was real life, and no change of heart was happening during commercial breaks.

The complex realities of blending a family came crashing home and, for a while, it seemed we would all fail. I became more obstinate and unbending as I grew weary of being a mediator. Charles withdrew, often heading to bed early and working weekends to avoid conflicts. Jeremy rebelled, hiding out in his bedroom, taking up smoking, skipping school, and allowing his grades to drop, before eventually choosing to live with his dad. Bekie immersed herself into a more constructive refuge … she overscheduled herself. This kept her from home as she joined the cheer squad, basketball team, and other school organizations. Though she made many friends and loved the activities, sadness was still evident in her eyes because of our struggles. Cali grew silent, biting her nails until they bled, plucking her eyelashes (from anxiety), and finally retreating into a fantasy life where she became a superhero through her reading and creative writing.

As I worried about Charles having second thoughts, I envisioned him leaving us for his former "good-time life." Pride kicked in, and to save him the trouble, I reluctantly but bluntly offered, "You don't have to stay. We made it before you came along, and we can make it again." Fortunately, Charles never took me up on that ridiculous offer. Yet, even I had days where I wanted to rewind the clock to just me and the kids, existing in our familiar routine as a single-parent family.

Our lives were in a major upheaval, and our attempts to blend our family were messy. Real people, raw emotions, hurtful behaviors, and foolish regret resided as we failed to call on our strongest advocate, God.

I can still recall the night that it all began to change. Charles and I had clashed in our positions, neither willing to budge. Overwhelmed, I stormed out of our home (the first time ever), packing a bag, placing him in charge of the kids while I spent the night in a local hotel as I contemplated my next steps. That night, I literally fell on my knees before the Lord. I pointed fingers at my husband and children. I cried, pouring my heart out before God.

I lay awake, praying and begging for His guidance. I was ready to shuck this stepfamily thing for good when God entered my thoughts and whispered to my heart. *It's you.*

"What? Not me," I argued. "I've given it my all. I've sacrificed and attempted to be the peacemaker, God. It's them! Are you sure you're looking at the right scenario? The right family?"

God remained steady throughout the night with His message to me. *It's you. Go home.*

"I can't." I replied.

That's your pride speaking. Go home. Love me first. Love your husband, and love your children. I'll guide you in this. Again, He spoke to my heart.

"But how?" I questioned. "I've tried to change them, and they just won't."

Then you change! came God's reply.

"What? Why me?" I asked.

God was silent after that, but His message continued to run through my head. I assume He was tired of arguing with my ignorance. He had spoken, He had guided, and now it was up to me to follow, or not.

The next day, I arose (though I never really slept) and returned home after a fretful day at work. Swallowing my pride in one of the most difficult moments in my life, I entered our home, where Charles waited. My anxiety and anticipation of how he would respond never materialized. He simply hugged me and said, "Welcome home, Darlin'." Three of the sweetest words I've ever heard.

The real-life Bradley Bunch began to solidify after that day. I prayed daily and worked to bring about the change in myself that was needed. As a result, Charles, too, began to change.

In going from three to five children, Charles learned that sometimes, despite your best efforts, children don't do and act as you wish. Rather than programmed little robots, children have minds of their own, strong and free wills, and they sometimes act in ways that make you cringe as a parent.

Charles grew more tolerant with the physical and emotional messiness of family. He introduced my children as his own, attending their school functions, encouraging their talents, and expressing his love and appreciation to and for them.

I prayed constantly, intervened less, and allowed Charles the respect and authority he deserved as a father. I quit straddling the fence and worked to have God dictate my response in trying situations (I'm still working at that!).

It wasn't an overnight process but small changes in our attitudes and actions began to make big differences in our blending as a family. As my three older children helped care for their two little brothers, they became less self-focused. They realized how hard Charles worked to provide our family with a stable living, something we'd struggled with in a single-parent home.

They observed him making the same demands of our boys as he did of them. They began to understand his style of parenting rather than seeing him as "picking on them." They began to show respect for his authority and our family rules. In fact, both of my daughters had him, along with their birth father, accompany them down the aisle at their weddings.

We all spent more time participating in each other's lives in positive ways—through church, prayer, travel, play, and laughter—and not just through imposing opinions and boundaries. Finally a family, we learned that the process requires more work than any television show—more patience, more tolerance, more giving, and much more prayer than the "script" calls for, to be exact. But we are finally a family. Through the mixing, stirring, and blending of our lives, emotions, needs, and wants, we've baked into a giant batch of messy love!

Blending a family *can* work. But prepare for better *and* worse, because both are going to happen. However you go into this, be sure to equip yourselves with prayer, diligence, commitment, and guidance from God. You can make it. He tells us that in Matthew 19:26, *"Jesus looked at them and said, 'With man this is impossible, but with God all things are possible'"* (ESV).

There will be struggles. There will be anger. There will be battles. There will be tears—rivers of them. And, if you're not up to dealing with those muddling emotional difficulties and seeking God's help, you are preparing for disaster. It's unfair to involve the emotions of your children … they have been "stirred" enough.

However, if you are willing to arm yourself with God's guidance in the parenting and blending of your family, God offers this wise counsel in Colossians 3:12-15, *"12 Put on then, as God's chosen ones, holy and beloved, compassionate hearts, kindness, humility, meekness, and patience, 13 bearing with one another and, if one has a complaint against another, forgiving each other; as the Lord has forgiven you, so you also must forgive. 14 And above all these put on love, which binds everything together in perfect harmony. 15 And let the peace of Christ rule in your hearts, to which indeed you were called in one body. And be thankful"* (ESV).

Other suggestions for blending your family from my own experience, as well as the advice of experts and friends, include the following tidbits:

Behavior: Be the adult and remain respectful, even if the children, or the ex-spouse/family aren't. Remember, you can't control how others behave, but you can control your response. As one friend shared, "Together, discuss and establish your role in decision making and discipline prior to marriage, and adjust as needed." It's important to encourage an amicable relationship between your ex and future/current spouse. It's also extremely critical not to downgrade or demean the ex-spouse or parent, especially in the children's presence. Work to resolve matters peacefully, with everyone's dignity intact.

Communication: Talk often with each other, with the children, and, if possible, with the ex-spouse, keeping him or her in the loop regarding appropriate children issues. Let your conversations be with regard. Speak and act in a way that says, "I respect and am choosing to love you," even when you don't feel it. Refuse to stoop to an ugly level if the other party becomes angry or acts in a hurtful way toward you. If you are about to behave in a regretful manner, walk away. Remove yourself and cool off as you pray for wisdom during these times. Put yourself in the child's shoes (and heart) to gain perspective.

Ask questions in a respectful, sincere, and receptive manner to resolve the issue.

Balance: Don't always be the "hammer." Balance responsibilities and expectations with playfulness and fun times. Have a sense of humor. Be willing to work alongside each other when chores are delegated. Be available, present, involved, and interested in the children's activities. Be flexible and don't insist on having things always go your way.

Memories: Create traditions and moments that cause you to bond as a blended family. Attempt to share special times without conflict by remaining flexible. Remember holidays are not a time to shuffle children from place to place or family to family just because the adults on all sides desire time with them. Make holidays more special and less stressful by allowing the children some say and determining not to pressure them with the demands of all. Attempt to create team parenting by negotiating and compromising with your ex-spouse regarding alternating holidays for the children's sake.

Awareness: Be wary of giving into children's demands or attempts to divide the family and/or pit you against your spouse, or even the ex-spouse. After all, when sparks fly, kids get caught in the middle and all get burned. Some children will retreat, striving to regain peace, even to the detriment of their own well-being. Others may attempt to get what they desire by pitting parents and/or families against each other, controlling decisions and emotions on both sides. Such actions may seem justified in children's minds as they feel victim to the circumstances that tore their world apart. Yet, if parents fall into this trap, they fuel the fire, causing greater conflict and chaos for all parties. So, be aware. Refuse to be a party to such behavior. Take time to lovingly listen and talk with your children about the dangers of this. Remain firm in doing the right thing. Though it's easier to cave just to keep the peace, it's very unhealthy for all. Instead, help your children be aware of their part in creating a healthy family structure.

Fairness: Refuse to show partiality. Not that you can't arrange for special dates with each child at different times, but beware of showing preferential treatment. While children may earn degrees of freedom based on wise choices and responsible behavior, be sure to explain how and why this is happening. Demonstrate unity, respect, patience, and love, even if/when you don't feel it. Introduce, treat, and work to love your stepchildren as your own.

Invest: Model righteousness, and act accordingly for everyone's sake, despite what others may do. Always invest in your children's lives, not just at your convenience or desire. After all, if you're only making demands rather than deposits, you probably won't earn the children's devotion. This will pay big dividends in the long run, though you may not see results for years.

Faith: When blending your family seems impossible, look to God, and believe. Be prepared to change yourself before worrying about changing anyone else.

As the Bradley Bunch continues to pray for guidance, especially with the addition of seven grandchildren (who share time/holidays with other families), we strive to keep our focus on God's plan for us, rather than our own selfish desires (still not easy!). It's been a rough road to develop a realistic vision of what our blended family should be, but God has inspired us to see what matters most as He guides us in the parenting/blended family process through His word.

Coaching Time

Consider the scriptures as you explore the five Cs of parenting in a blended family: Communication, Caring, Commitment, Consideration and Celebration.

1. **Communication:** How are you making time to talk about what's happening in your children's lives, what's important, and what you all might need from each other in an environment that is honest, open, respectful, and kind?

    "Let no corrupting talk come out of your mouths, but only such as is good for building up, as fits the occasion, that it may give grace to those who hear."

    Ephesians 4:29 ESV

    "A gentle answer turns away wrath, but a harsh word stirs up anger."

    Proverbs 15:1 NIV

2. **Caring:** How are you demonstrating love for each other through words and deeds? What needs to change and how and when will that happen?

    "Let each of you look not only to his own interests, but also to the interests of others."

    Philippians 2:4 ESV

"Be kind to one another, tenderhearted, forgiving one another, as Christ forgave you."

Ephesians 4:32 ESV

3. **Commitment:** How can your actions demonstrate an unselfish focus on God first, and then family before self? Psalm 37:5 ESV

   "Commit your way to the Lord; trust in Him and He will act."

   Psalm 37:5 ESV

   "Commit your work to the Lord, and your plans will be established."

   Proverbs 16:3 ESV

4. **Consideration:** How will you bear the burdens of each other? In what ways can you encourage, help, and support each other? How will you "be there" for each other in a way that matters?

   "12 Now we ask you, brothers and sisters, to acknowledge those who work hard among you, who care for you in the Lord and who admonish you. 13 Hold them in the highest regard in love because of their work. Live in peace with each other."

   1 Thessalonians 5:12-13 ESV

   So then, while we have opportunity, let us do good to all people, and especially to those who are of the household of the faith."

   Galatians 6:10 ESV

5. **Celebration:** How will you make time to actively enjoy God, appreciate time with your children/family, as well as celebrate each other's successes and progress?

"You make known to me the path of life; in your presence there is fullness of joy; at your right hand are pleasures forevermore."

Psalm 16:11 ESV

"Also that everyone should eat and drink and take pleasure in all his toil—this is God's gift to man."

Ecclesiastes 3:13 ESV

Prayer: *Lord, be with me in this blended parenting process. It can be so difficult, so harsh for all involved. It's so easy to fall away from your path when emotions are heated. I grow weary of trying to do the right things—especially when others can be so hurtful. I need your guidance. Give me wisdom, patience, and tolerance to do your will. Help me to serve as a strong, forgiving, and loving example of what a parent should be, not only for my/our children, but for all family members involved in this journey as they, too, have influence on our children. In your name, I pray. Amen.*

Poem: This poem was written the first year I was unable to spend a holiday with all of my family as my children were scattered. It serves as a reminder of just how precious family is … both the "blended" and the "blood."

Family

Family. Those people who are an extension of you. They bring out the worst in you and they bring out the best in you. Yet, it is family who continues to love you.

Family. The warmth that pulses through your veins and keeps you connected. Despite distance. Despite differences. Despite difficulties. It's family that makes your blood boil and family that fills your empty heart.

Family. The connection you often take for granted, yet appreciate most. They can dismiss you with a glance, then lift you with a kiss. More than kin, they are bonded to your being.

Family. Those people who see through you, stand by you, and reach past all barriers to support you when you need it most. They recognize your weaknesses, yet build upon your strengths.

Family. The relationship that goes far beyond any friendship. Beyond love. Beyond acceptance. Beyond forgiveness.. It goes to a place deep in the heart that only family can understand.

Family. That part which is sacred and holy to your soul. That attachment which is vital to making life precious and meaningful. It is a completion that cannot be explained, only experienced. It is that wholeness God meant for us to know.

Chapter 8

THE ONGROWING JOURNEY ...

"I have no greater joy than to hear that my children are walking in the truth."

3 John 1:4 ESV

"Devote yourselves to prayer, being watchful and thankful... Be wise in the way you act toward outsiders; make the most of every opportunity. Let your conversation be always full of grace, seasoned with salt, so that you may know how to answer everyone."

Colossians 4:2, 5-6 NIV

My purpose as a parent is to continually keep my children close to God. It is not by accident that they develop into and continue to be the people God meant them to be. Yet, because my children are now grown, my status as a parent has changed. As young adults, my children love me, but they no longer need me as they once did. Seldom requiring help or advice, they go about their business consumed with school, work, and/or families of their own.

While involvement *with* and prayers *for* my children are continual, my interventions and guidance are not. Letting them go and watching them grow can be a difficult and emotional transition.

As I relegate myself to the lesser role, I'm still quick to seize those occasional instances to support my children through that just-right scripture, message, or action. Bearing in mind no life or well-being is immediately at risk, my general rule is to trust my children to do the right things or to await their invitation for input. However, as I remain aware of their needs, I am alert to God's directive when He calls for intervention. No simple task, this requires love, boldness, patience, wisdom and humility, accomplished only through God's assistance.

But how can we know when such intercession is being called for by God? Discernment is key as Philippians 1:9-10 tells us: *"And this is my prayer: that your love may abound more and more in knowledge and depth of insight, so that you may be able to discern what is best and may be pure and blameless until the day of Christ, filled with the fruit of righteousness that comes through Jesus Christ – to the glory and praise of God."* (ESV).

So, first and always, pray! Such moments, or should I say *all* moments, require prayer. Next, ask yourself three questions: 1) Is my intention aligned with God's word? 2) Will my involvement help my child in the right ways (i.e. to grow better and/or healthier as a person and Christian)? and, 3) Will my intervention prevent my child or someone else from being hurt or lost? If the answer to any or all of those questions is yes, it's time to take action in a loving, but God-like manner.

Prepare for the best way to go about it. Put your own emotions and pride aside. Lovingly work to keep judgment out and the dignity of all intact. Consider your child's personality and what approach may work best. And, as much as possible, allow for time to do it right. This means capitalizing on reflection, prayer, a search of the scriptures and an opportunity to seek the counsel of God's people—those trusted confidantes from your village—before acting.

Will a comment or a conversation do the job? Or, is firm, immediate action required? What reinforcements or outside resources might be necessary? Remember, prayer, preparation and a positive approach work wonders during this time!

It is also wise to arrange ahead for possible consequences. When your efforts are uninvited, you can bet your intervention may well be unappreciated. This may possibly affect your relationship with your children in a negative way. At other times, or even later down the road, your children may gratefully acknowledge your wisdom, support and courage for doing what was best for them. And, should your children become resentful, take comfort in knowing you did what God called you to do. That is sufficient.

That's not to say we have permission to interfere in our adult children's lives with a self-focused, know-it-all, pitiful-me approach either. Such unhealthy inclinations may alienate our adult children and/or their significant others. Fortunately, these attitudes are easily recognized and readily remedied when we align our conduct with God's will. Take a moment to examine these characteristics. Can you identify with any of these behaviors? I know I did!

- **Guilt Goading:** This is when self-focused desires keep us from seeing the big picture. We fail to recognize life's demands on our children. This is reflected in comments such as, *"Why don't you ever call me? What do you mean you won't be spending Christmas with me?! No one visits me anymore. My grandchildren won't even know who I am!"*

- **Financial Follies:** This practice goes both ways. Either we as parents expect our children to provide for us financially *and/or* we continue to provide financial assistance for them, despite them being capable of earning their own way. This is considered enabling, by the way, not empowering. Statements may be subtle or blatantly obvious, *"The kids really need a new laptop for school but I just can't afford it right now. I'm considering buying a new car and I was wondering if you could help by paying the insurance for me."*

- **Constant Critiquing:** No explanation needed here … just a reminder not to be Nagging Nellie or Negative Ned! Such damaging remarks might be, *"Can't you get a better paying job? Your house is a pit! You've put on quite a bit of weight lately; are you exercising?! Your spouse is awfully rude."*

- **Arrogant Authority/Advice:** This is that know-it-all, I-did-it-better counsel that is uninvited and unnecessary, but so easy to offer! *"You do realize that's a waste of your money and time. If you don't discipline your children, I will! When I was your age, I did it all …worked full time, raised three children and managed a house, all while going to night school. I told you so but you just wouldn't listen."*

Go back and read these a second time. Be honest. Which of these approaches have you used with your grown children? I'm afraid I'm guilty of all four!

What might be a better tactic? Rather than making the situation about you and your emotions, make it about what's best for all involved. Before speaking or acting, ask yourself, is this worth it? Will my words or behavior cause undue damage to this relationship?

Be proactive. Instead of complaining about not having enough time with your children, take the initiative to do something about it. Words are cheap (and often harmful). Arrange to visit them. Attend one of their events and take them out to dinner.

Instead of whining about the respect and love owed you, give both to your children unconditionally. Model what you desire. Practice what you preach. Walk the talk. These may be old adages but they get proven results.

Once you've recognized what needs to change, prayerfully seek God's guidance. To continue as a significant presence in your adult children's lives, seek the scriptures to address issues appropriately. After all, it's not what you say as much as how you say it to your children. Or maybe it's what you *don't* say that matters most.

When Bekie had her first child, Atley, it wasn't long before we realized he was different. Handsome and loveable, he had an extremely high intellect, but he became emotionally distraught when things did not go his way. He had sensory issues when it came to food or clothing textures, refusing to eat or wear certain things. We all thought he was just being spoiled. So, by the time Atley was five, my husband and

I, along with other well-meaning relatives, offered tons of advice as to how Bekie should handle him. Our uninvited authority especially backfired when we took it upon ourselves to discipline him.

While visiting our home, Atley threw the ball across the room, despite being told not to do so earlier. Rather than giving Bekie a chance to take action, my husband stepped in. Charles was going to show my daughter how to get results. In a harsh voice, Charles scolded Atley, placing him firmly in the corner for time out. Then he proceeded to tell Bekie how Atley was getting out of hand.

In just a matter of minutes, everyone was crying, including me! Atley wailed, Bekie wiped humiliated tears from her cheeks, and Charles sat with arms folded tightly across his chest, his face red with frustration. As his eyes searched my face for answers, I just shook my head and shrugged. Refusing to let the situation fester, Charles took action. He offered an apology and hug to Atley and Bekie, and fortunately, both were quick to forgive. It was an emotional fiasco, but one from which we all learned.

Charles and I realized that day that the way we had disciplined our children wasn't working with Atley. We learned Bekie's way of handling him was far more effective. What we didn't know is why. But that came to us a couple of years later, when God laid it on my heart to intervene in a different way.

As an educator working with thousands of children over my extended career, I knew Atley had challenges. Bekie saw it too, and as a certified teacher, she had chosen to homeschool because of his needs. She and her husband had done many things to help Atley, but often, they were seen as "bad parents" when Atley had his emotional meltdowns.

Finally, after much prayer (and a consultation with my sister, Hope, a social worker) I called my daughter. Bekie and I discussed the pros and cons of testing Atley, focusing on all the possible resources available to best address his challenges. After prayer and conversation with her husband, Bekie decided on the testing, and not surprisingly, Atley was found to have moderate to high-functioning autism.

What a relief this was! Not just for us, but for Atley. Now we have an understanding of why food textures and certain interactions cause him to become so distressed. We recognize we cannot respond to him like we might with others. Thankfully, Bekie continues to do her own research on autism, and she shares with us how we can all work best with Atley.

It's important to remember that despite our best intentions as parents, we will have those moments where we muddle things. We're just human. When this happens, we cannot afford to wallow in self-hate or pity. We cannot dwell in a prideful mode. Destructive emotions serve no purpose. Life is too short to spend in regret or isolation. None of us will ever reach perfection on this earth. Not as a person. Not as a parent.

Instead we must learn from those times and grow better. We must be willing to acknowledge our mistakes, apologize for them, and refuse to reside there.

Through a thoughtful, deliberate and intentional process, we can equip our brains and hearts for such moments by learning God's word. Then, as challenges arise, we can respond lovingly, through a habit of the spirit, allowing respect to replace authority, unselfish regard to overcome demands; trust to substitute for prideful advice, and a hopeful countenance to replace criticism.

As a parent, you have the power to be an influential force in your children's lives. Just don't be the bulldozer. Continue creating the relationships you desire with your children. Make deposits so when you must make a withdrawal, something is left in that emotional bank.

Invest time. Bestow love. Celebrate this chance to learn from the past, live in the present, and plan for the future with your children and grandchildren. After all, as Psalm 127:3 reminds us, *"Children are a gift and reward from the Lord"* (NLT). Hold your Father's hand as you journey through this magnificent privilege.

Coaching Time

As you reflect and pray, allow the following questions to keep you on track throughout your parenting journey.

1. When intervention is necessary with your adult children, how will you discern the best way to go about it? What village people and resources will help?

2. How will you maintain a healthy involvement without intruding in your adult children's lives?

3. Consider the characteristics and behaviors that may alienate your children from you. What can/will you do to change?

4. How will you stay connected to God in your parenting endeavors? In what ways will you monitor and measure your ongoing development?

Prayer: *Lord, thank you for my blessings and the many years spent guiding my children with your word. What a wondrous privilege and honor this role has been! Give me wisdom to discern your voice from my emotions when there is a need for intervention. Help me to continue to serve as a positive model and mentor for my children and their families. Guide my children to be the parents you meant them to be. Let my life be a testament to your word. As a parent, grandparent and Christian, help me to love, forgive, and live in a manner that glorifies your name and serves your purpose. In your name, I pray. Amen.*

Poem: This is a poem written and dedicated to me by my children for Christmas in 2013. It's one of my favorite Christmas gifts ever, and a testament to the importance of holding my Father's hand on this parenting journey!

The Journey with Mom …

Mom, Over the years you have taught us so many things:
When storms come … dance in the rain.
When you have the chance … laugh 'til you cry!
If you get knocked down … get back up.
When lost … pray.
When hungry …EAT! A French fry won't kill you.
When numb … smile until you feel it.
When down … count your blessings.
When hope is buried … find family —they will dig it up.

Holding My Father's Hand: Faith-based Parenting

When you need help ... Ask. Family will always be there.
When wronged ... forgive and forget.
When there is a choice ... always stand up for what's right, even against the odds.
When life's music plays ... dance!
Be positive ... it's contagious!
Be confident ... it's attractive.
If you're not going to poop ... get off the pot.
Don't be afraid to be different ... it's refreshing.
In all you do ... have fun—life is short.
Live in the moment ...not in the past.
Honor your name ... your reputation follows you.
Respect your elders ... and they will respect you.
Don't worry ... your life is in God's hands.
Create your own path ... ignore common stereotypes and assumptions.
Choose your friends wisely ... they will lift you up or pull you down.
Always remember ... Love should make you a better person.
Believe you can do it ... and you can!
Learn from mistakes ... they are God's lessons.
Do it right the first time ... or you will have to do it again.
It's not the size of the bat ... but the swing that counts.
Go for the impossible ... you just might get it.
Give 100% ... or get off the field.
Don't be afraid to dream ... and never give up on your dreams.
Don't be afraid to speak your mind ... and be true to what you believe.
Your gifts are from God ... so use them to honor Him.
When afraid ... let go and let God.
Love each other ... be faithful and be present
Whether you think you can or think you can't ... you're right.
In this family, you will never walk through life alone because ...
with God and family,
Ain't No Mountain High Enough!

Appendix

Research and Survey Data Results

The most important guidance for this book came from prayer, scripture, and my own experiences (what I did right and wrong as a parent). Because my role as a school leader is so similar to my role as a parent, I decided to tap into the same characteristics identified in my relationship with students which correlated with good parenting.

Although research tells us that a parent/family member can be the most influential person in a child's life, I decided to administer my own informal survey to see how it compares. My purpose was to determine which of the parents' actions were the most influential in the lives of survey participants. I also wanted to gather participants' definitions of a "good parent." This data was desegregated and then used to guide the direction of my book.

Created on Survey Monkey, this nine-item questionnaire (both open-ended and multiple choice) allowed all participants to remain anonymous. The survey link was disseminated in the following ways:

- facebook
- email
- text message
- word of mouth

Most of the eighty-six survey participants were from Oklahoma, although the survey was also shared with residents of Texas, Arizona, Kansas, and beyond. Many of those taking the survey passed the link on to colleagues, friends, and family. A text analysis allowed me to group "like" answers from the open-ended responses. The survey questions included:

1. List 3-5 significant things that you/your parents did that had a positive influence on you and/or your child's life and character. In other words, what did you/your parents do right as parents?

2. List 3-5 things you wish you and/or your parents would have done differently in parenting.

3. Are you a parent and/or step parent?

    - Yes
    - No

4. What is your gender?

    - Female
    - Male

5. What are the ages of your child(ren)?

6. What is the gender of your child(ren)?

7. Which of the following best describes your current relationship status?

    - Married

Appendix

- Widowed
- Divorced
- Separated
- In a Domestic partnership
- Single but cohabitating
- Single, never married

8. What is your definition of good parenting?

9. Do you have any comments you'd like to add to this parenting survey?

RESULTS OF THE SURVEY:

The results are below. Using Text Analysis to group like answers, only the top six are listed, starting with the most popular. Some of the questions' percentages do not total 100 percent because many questions were open-ended rather than multiple choice.

In question one, participants were asked to list those positive things parents did that influenced their lives and character. Forty-nine percent mentioned parents' presence, involvement, and creating family time as substantial factors. Forty-four percent of the participants felt that parents sharing God, faith (godly influence, example, and prayers), and attending church made a difference for them. Boundaries and expectations (along with discipline, consequences) were named as being a major factor by 35 percent of the participants.

Another 29 percent named the parent behaving as a model and/or example as important, while 27 percent mentioned parents providing them with responsibilities and work or chores as significant. Last, but not least, 26 percent listed a parent's demonstration of love and/or unconditional love as a factor.

In question two, participants were asked what they wished their parents would have done differently in parenting. The majority of responses (30 percent) named their parents' lack of presence, involvement, or time spent with them. 24 percent mentioned the failure or process of communication about real life issues as a factor. The third most named factor, at 24 percent, was the failure of parents to make their children responsible or more self-sufficient. Twenty percent of the participants listed their parents' lack of love and affection, while 15 percent named failure to provide a peaceful home life as significant.

Questions three and four revealed 87 percent of respondents were parents or stepparents and 78 percent of the respondents were female.

The predominant age(s) of respondents' children (question five) fell into the 18+ age group (62 percent). 19 percent of their children were school-age, and 19 percent of their children fell into both age categories. 8 percent of the participants answered they did not have children, but responded according to how they were parented.

In question six, the survey showed the predominant gender of the respondents' children as male (24 percent), with 20 percent female and 48 percent of the respondents having both genders. 8 percent of the participants had no children.

Question seven disclosed 76 percent of participants as married, 10 percent as divorced/separated, 8 percent as single or never married, 3 percent as co-habitating, and 1 percent as widowed. 2 percent failed to answer.

For question eight, participants were asked to define good parenting. 53 percent mentioned love/unconditional love as the most important characteristic. 37 percent mentioned serving as a role model/example, 31 percent listed factors such as encouraging, supportive and nurturing, while 27 percent stated that teaching children character and respect were significant attributes. 26 percent shared that teaching God, demonstrating faith and providing spiritual guidance were important while 20 percent identified consistency, stability, and safety. Finally, 20 percent listed teaching children responsibility and the ability to be self-reliant as necessities.

The last question allowed respondents to offer comments in addition to their answers. Forty-eight participants provided various responses.

Making Sense of the Data: My Interpretation

Presence: The number one answer to question one was for parents to be involved—to be *there* for their children, to be truly present. In addition, respondents named having parents as role models, as well as parents who made time for family matters as two of the top six ways parents positively influenced them during their growing-up years. Travel, vacations, family rituals, play, laughter, and fun together were also named as positive indicators.

God/Faith/Church: This was the second highest response to survey question one. Respondents discussed the influence of their parents as Christian examples/role models, as well as going to church, praying together, and sharing scriptures and faith. Participants also stated they wished parents had been more open and communicative about their beliefs and God's word.

Boundaries and Expectations: In two of the survey questions, one asking respondents what they wished their parents (or they) had done differently, and the second asking what their parents had done right in the parenting process, the answers were the same: Parents instilling a sense of responsibility and appreciation in their children through hard work and allowing them to grow from challenges and hardships, rather than rescuing them made a difference.

Communication/Listening: The second-highest response to the survey question, "What do you wish your parents (or you as a parent) had done differently in the parenting process?" was listening! Respondents stated they wish their parents had truly listened to them—with eye contact, full presence and interest, and undivided attention. In addition, they had desired their parents talk with them openly and honestly about important life issues, including dating, sex, alcoholism, drug abuse, finances, relationships, and divorce. Finally, they preferred more loving guidance regarding education, grades, and potential career choices.

Unconditional Love and Peace: Respondents said they wish their parents had been more verbal and demonstrative with their affection. More "I love yous and more hugs (yes, body language is a form of communication, too!!). Less criticism and more encouragement.

Appendix

More verbal celebrations of their successes and peaceful conversations over yelling and/or fighting (parent to parent as well as parent to child).

Resources/References

Bruner, Kurt. "Putting God First." *Thriving Family*, Accessed September 10, 2014, http://www.thrivingfamily.com/Family/Faith/2010/apr/putting-god-first.aspx

Churchill, Winston S. *Never Give In! The Best of Winston Churchill's Speeches*. New York: Hachette Books, 2004.

Dr. Seuss, *Horton Hatches the Egg*, New York: Random House, 1968.

Dunnewold, Ann. *Even June Cleaver Would Forget the Juice Box*. Deerfield Beach: Health Communications, Inc., 2007.

English Standard Version Bible: Containing the Old and New Testaments with Apocrypha. Oxford: Oxford UP, 2009. Print.

Ginott, Haim G. *Teacher and Child: A Book for Parents and Teachers*. New York: Scribner Paper Fiction, 1993.

New International Version. [Colorado Springs]: Biblica, 2011. *BibleGateway.com*. Web. 3 Mar. 2011.

Wolff, Karen. "Raising Kids God's Way: Passing on Your Faith to Your Children." Accessed November 15, 2014, *About.com*. http://christianity.about.com/od/parentingresources/a/raisekids4god.htm

Zondervan NIV Study Bible. Fully rev. ed. Kenneth L. Barker, gen. ed. Grand Rapids: Zondervan, 2002. Print

Contact Information:
Email: pambradley7@gmail.com
or bradley.pamela7@yahoo.com
Website: pambradley.net